HELP YOUR CHILD be Confident

A PARENTS' HANDBOOK

Clare Shaw

The Publishers would like to thank the children of Charlbury Primary School, Oxfordshire, for their help with the covers for this series.

A catalogue record for this publication is available from the British Library.

ISBN 0 340 67004 5

First published 1996
Impression number 10 9 8 7 6 5 4 3 2 1
Year 1999 1998 1997 1996

Typeset by Wearset, Boldon, Tyne and Wear.
Printed in Great Britain for Hodder & Stoughton Educational, a division of Hodder Headline Plc, 338 Euston Road, London NW1 3BH by Cox and Wyman Ltd, Reading, Berks.

Positive Parenting

Positive parenting is a series of handbooks primarily written for parents, in a clear, accessible style, giving practical information, sound advice and sources of specialist and general help. Based on the authors' extensive professional and personal experience, they cover a wide range of topics and provide an invaluable source of encouragement and information to all who are involved in child care in the home and in the community.

Other books in this series include:

Talking and your child 0 340 57526 3 by Clare Shaw – a guide outlining the details of how speech and language develops from birth to age 11 and how parents can help with the process.

Your child from 5–11 0 340 54750 2 by Jennie and Lance Lindon – a guide showing parents how they can help their children through these crucial early years, stressing the contribution a caring family can make to the emotional, physical and intellectual development of the child.

Help your child through school 0 340 60796 3 by Jennie and Lance Lindon – a guide which looks at the school years from the perspective of the family, showing how parents can help their children to get the most out of their years at primary school and how to ease the transition into secondary education.

Help your child with maths 0 340 60767 X by Sue Atkinson – a comprehensive guide to show parents how they can help develop their children's mathematical awareness and confidence from babyhood through the primary years and into secondary school.

Help your child with reading and writing 0 340 60768 8 by Lesley Clark – a guide which describes the stages children go through when learning to read and write and shows parents how they can encourage and enjoy their children's early development in these vital areas.

Prepare your child for school 0 340 60797 1 by Clare Shaw – a very practical guide for parents whose children are about to start school.

Help your child with a foreign language 0 340 60766 1 by Opal Dunn – written for all parents, including those who do not speak a foreign language, this guide examines the right time to start teaching a child a foreign language, how to begin, and how to progress to fluency.

Teenagers in the family 0 340 62106 0 by Debi Roker and John Coleman of the Trust for Adolescence covers all the major issues that parents face as their children pass through the turbulent teenage years, such as rules and regulations, setting boundaries, communication, decision making, risky behaviour, health issues, and problems at school.

Teenagers and sexuality 0 340 62105 2 by John Coleman of the Trust for Adolescence gives practical advice for parents who are finding it difficult to talk to their teenagers about sex and who need help to understand, and deal with, their teenagers' emerging sexuality.

Help your child with homework and exams 0 340 65866 5 by Jennie Lindon offers parents practical advice on how they can help their children to take a positive approach to homework and exams across the whole school curriculum.

Help your child through the National Curriculum 0 340 66936 5 by Graeme Kent shows how parents can help their primary school children cope with, and enjoy, the subjects of the National Curriculum and prepare for Key Stage 1 and 2 Assessment Tests (taken at the ages of 7 and 11).

Contents

Introduction

All parents would like their children to be happy, have plenty of friends, find life as easy and enjoyable as possible and achieve their potential, tackling life's challenges with optimism and success. In other words, to be confident children. This does not mean we want to change our children for different ones or that we want them to have totally different personalities. We want them just as they are but with added confidence. Confident children come with a range of personalities and do not have to be outgoing and gregarious – the life and soul of the party. All children are different whatever their confidence level and many will be quietly confident rather than extrovertly confident.

If we are to accept our children for what they are, perhaps we should then accept that some children are not confident and allow them to be that way. But all children have the potential to be confident and we would be doing them a great disservice if we sat back and let them struggle on with low self-confidence, poor self-esteem or no feeling of self-worth. Children lacking in confidence can find life very difficult indeed. It affects every area of their life and often means that they fall short of their true potential.

Very few children, or adults, are confident all the time. We all have areas of our lives when our confidence seems to abandon us.

As children grow, there will be particular times in their lives when they need an extra boost of confidence to get them through – and this is where a parent comes in. Parents have the potential to spot when confidence is low or lacking and to do something about it. We cannot protect our children from all the ups and downs life brings but we can give our children enough confidence to cope. This book shows you how.

Throughout this book the child is referred to as 'she' and 'he' in alternate chapters, although the information is obviously applicable to boys and girls. My own experience is of bringing up two daughters. One seemed to be born with an inner confidence while the other needed help for her confidence to grow. The ideas in this book have therefore been tried and tested to very good effect. Although other counsellors, psychologists and psychiatrists were consulted in the writing of this book, the real experts were the parents who had 'been through it' and kindly told me their stories, some of which are included in this book.

Hopefully, with the help of these guidelines and a lot of determination, you too can give your child the confidence that he or she deserves.

CHAPTER ONE

What is confidence?

Even before a baby is born, parents have hopes about what she will be like and what the future holds for her. Amongst these hopes, happiness comes top of everyone's list. How many new parents say 'I just want her to be happy'? And what does that really mean? By happiness we really mean that we want life to be easy for our children, that we want it to be free of difficulties and that we want them to enjoy life. Self-esteem and confidence are very closely linked in our minds with happiness. And so they should be. A child who feels good about herself is more likely to feel happy more of the time. Research has shown that a child with high self-esteem copes better with stress and difficulty when they arise and is less likely to get into 'trouble'. When we think of the happy children that we know, we think of the popular, outgoing, confident ones and not the quiet, shy children left on the sidelines on their own. When we wish happiness upon our children we include confidence and a strong ability to make friends and be liked.

A confident child is one who finds life easier. She feels good about herself and so copes with new people and situations with ease. Part of feeling good about herself is accepting herself, warts and all. She may well be aware of her faults, or imperfections in appearance, but she accepts them and does not let them stop her getting on with life.

Where does assertiveness fit in?

A confident child is fully assured and self-reliant and is likely to have a good opinion of herself – or a high self-esteem. To be assertive is to be able to insist on your rights and opinions. Clearly, in order to be assertive you need both confidence and a high self-esteem. It is often adults lacking in these traits who tend to go on assertiveness courses, which have increased in popularity over the past few years. A child is still learning what her rights are and will be forming new opinions about everything as she develops. Assertiveness is therefore more applicable to the older child or teenager. Even so, a child can learn from a very early age if her opinions are important and listened to by others – especially her parents. Listening to your child's views on, say, where you go on holiday or even what you have for tea and not putting them down or dismissing them should help with assertiveness later in life. Of course, this does not mean you always have to do as your child suggests – just that you take her suggestions seriously.

Can children be too confident?

As long as a child has concern for others and an awareness that nobody, including herself, is perfect, she cannot be too confident. However, someone who is completely oblivious to any of her faults and short-comings may have tipped over into arrogance or cockiness. An over-confident child may even become oblivious to danger, trusting everyone and every situation. We all know the difference between the quietly confident child and the cocky show-off. It is important to give our children just the right amount of confidence and self-esteem together with an awareness and concern for others. However, no child is perfect and we must accept that there will be periods when our confident child either momentarily loses her self-esteem or appears to become over-confident. This may be triggered by a particular age or stage in her life or else by a traumatic or difficult event.

Why is confidence so important?

Children with low self-esteem and low confidence are likely to under-achieve. They do not believe that they can succeed at something and so they do not. Children lacking in confidence find it difficult to form relationships with both adults and children and can find new situations difficult to deal with. As parents, we have to give far more support to children who lack confidence but we should be aware of the danger of over-protecting them by avoiding difficult or new situations altogether. Confidence enables a child to know herself, like herself and become more and more independent. When life becomes difficult, children with a high self-esteem will cope better.

Confidence is important for children but it is equally important for parents. We need to feel confident in our abilities as parents to cope with the difficult stages in our children's lives. Parental confidence will help us from blaming ourselves or feeling negative about what may be quite normal developmental stages such as toddler temper tantrums or moody teenage years.

Do we always know when our child is feeling confident?

There are two aspects of confidence – confident behaviour and confident feelings. If we feel confident, we are more likely to behave in a confident manner. However, as adults, we will have experienced many situations when we have felt a total lack of confidence and yet have managed to put on a brave face and act confidently. We may even fool others into thinking that we are totally confident in a difficult situation although our body language and non-verbal communication are likely to give us away. Very young children are less likely to try to cover up any feelings of low confidence unless we have made too much of being confident. It is essential therefore to introduce confidence in a non-pressurised way. We also need to be aware of the non-verbal signs of low confidence so that we can give the support and reassurance that are needed.

Signs of low confidence

Posture and body position This is the most obvious sign to look for. A confident child sits or walks in an upright position, shoulders back, head upright and looking straight ahead. A lack of confidence will show itself in a slumped body position, head bent, looking down. A confident child may walk ahead of you while a child lacking in confidence may walk behind you or even hide in your skirts. Look out for signs that your child would rather not be there – sitting on the edge of her chair or even looking at the door.

Eye contact Avoiding eye contact with the person she is speaking to indicates a lack of confidence.

Facial expression Look out for the 'false smile'. A child may put a smile on for show when she is really anxious underneath. This smile will not spread to the eyes and will be closed or show fewer teeth than normal.

Hands If your child is feeling nervous or unsure, then she is more likely to fiddle with her hands. She may fiddle with part of her clothing or even her hair. Her hands may wander across her mouth frequently, meaning that she does not want to talk.

Individual habits Thumb sucking or nail biting may be your child's way of seeking self-comfort when the going gets tough.

Tone of voice A child lacking in confidence may have a flatter tone to her voice. It may even quaver a little if she is nervous.

We all know how a confident child behaves – she walks into the room with her head up, initiating conversation and responding to any communication aimed at her. She seems happy to be there and acts as if she belongs. But how does a child with low confidence behave? Typically, we think of the shy child who looks as if she does not belong, avoids communication and stands on the sidelines, not joining in. However, low confidence can manifest itself in other ways too. Some children may actually become rather silly or even giggly while others may be rude or aggressive. These last two behaviours are typical of children who can be confident but have found a particular situation just too difficult to cope with. It may seem natural to reassure the obviously nervous child but, if she is being silly or rude, it may feel more natural to reprimand her. Of course, she needs to know that such behaviour is unacceptable, but you should consider the reasons for it. If she is nervous, she may also need reassurance and understanding. Whatever a child's reaction to a new situation, parents should respond in much the same way – with reassurance and understanding.

What should we expect?

Only a very few adults are confident in every situation. Most of us find new situations at least slightly daunting so it would be unrealistic to expect our children to be brimming over with confidence all the time. After all, they have many more new situations to cope with from the first day at a new school to a first date with a partner of the opposite sex. They have to learn to be confident as they develop and may need props to start with – perhaps the presence of a parent or even a special toy. Within this process of developing confidence there will be specific times when confidence will be put to the test. This may include individual traumas such as moving house or parents separating. But for all children there are particular stages of development, from the clinging eighteen-month-old toddler to the moody teenager, when confidence can temporarily wane. By being prepared for stages of low confidence, parents can act promptly with some confidence-boosting strategies. However, it must be remembered that all children are different and will not react to a situation in a stereotypical way.

At a glance: A guide to confident ages

0–2 years

Your baby is still learning that she is a separate individual and will not yet be giving herself specific attributes such as 'clever' or 'naughty'. She is unlikely to be affected in the long term by being told that she behaves badly but may be upset at the time. She is very tied to the here and now and is egocentric, believing that life revolves around her. Confidence, or a lack of it, is not yet established although parental habits may be. A clingy stage is likely which affects confident behaviour.

2–5 years

Your child is still egocentric but keen to please you. She may begin to take any criticisms to heart and will respond to praise and encouragement from parents. Your child will have to learn to cope with many new experiences including school and therefore increased independence. A high self-esteem can be established during these years.

5–12 years

Your child will develop a self-image during the early school years, giving herself labels such as 'good at art' or 'cheeky'. Some of these self-concepts will be based on labels given to her by other people including family and friends. Changing self-image and therefore self-esteem becomes increasingly difficult as your child matures.

12–18 years

During the adolescent years, children review what sort of person they are. They may have adopted certain characteristics to please you and may now challenge them to find out what sort of person they want to be. Mood swings can affect confidence and changes in appearance may affect self-esteem. These are challenging years for parents' own confidence in their parenting skills.

Why are some children more confident than others?

As parents of young babies will agree, we are born with some of our personal attributes already in place. A baby seems to have an individual personality right from the start and within days parents are talking about their 'placid baby' or perhaps their 'demanding baby'. Is confidence perhaps then something we are born with or is it just the effect of our upbringing and early experiences? The answer seems to be that both are important. Recent research has found a gene common to shy people and has found that a shy parent is more likely to have a shy child. However, even if a child is born with a predisposition to be confident, it is also clear that early experiences have an effect. Psychologists agree that a child who is overly criticised will not have as much confidence as a child who is praised and encouraged. This seems like common sense, but what else makes some children more confident than others?

Position in the family

There are some generalisations to be made about the position your child has in the family, whether she is an only, eldest, middle or youngest child. However, every family is different and personality is not entirely dependent on whether you have younger or older siblings.

Generally, only children are confident and self-assured. Their high self-esteem may be due to being the sole recipients of parental praise but they may be more confident in the company of adults than with other children.

Only and eldest children may be perfectionists and also anxious. This seems to be because parents pass on their anxiety of being a first-time parent. Generally then, elder children, like only children, are confident but anxiety can get in the way.

Middle children tend to make friends easily so are usually confident with their peer group. However, they often receive the least attention from adults which can lead to a lower self-esteem. They do not rely on parental approval and praise.

Youngest children are usually confident and easy going. However, they are eager to please parents and need a lot of praise and encouragement.

Parent tips

- Try to spend time with each of your children on their own – even ten minutes can help them to feel special.
- Make sure that an only child becomes confident in the company of other children by inviting friends home frequently.
- Are you allowing your youngest child to grow up? Some youngest children are 'babied' by the rest of the family and can then lack confidence when they start school or have to become more independent.
- Do not compare your child with her brothers and sisters or even her friends. Never catch yourself saying 'I wish you were more like . . .' or 'Why can't you be more like your brother?'

Physical differences

Some children may look different from other children and this may involve something seemingly trivial like a big nose or something more obvious such as a birthmark. At certain stages in a child's life it is important for her to conform and to look like other children of that age group. Anything, however trivial it may seem to us, which makes that child feel different will affect self-esteem. How the difference has been dealt with is important. To draw a lot of attention to it may make the child self-conscious but so may brushing it aside as totally unimportant, leaving the child to dwell on it alone. Focusing on the child's attributes is usually the best approach and enables many children with physical differences to have a good self-image.

Parent tips

- If your child has something which concerns her and which can be helped or cured, then arrange help. For example, a visit to the orthodontist is needed for a child who is self-conscious about sticking out teeth.
- Help your child to accentuate her attributes. For example, get a really good, flattering hair style for a child worried about a large nose.
- Make sure it is your child who is concerned and not you. If your child is not at all concerned about sticking out ears, then why mention them?
- A bully will pick on vulnerable and weak children; the fact that they are overweight or wear glasses is not the critical factor. A bully will always find something to make fun of. Contact the school and teach your child to deal with bullying with the help of Kidscape (address at back of the book).
- Focus on your child's personal attributes which are not linked to appearance. Perhaps she is helpful or kind to animals. Do not talk endlessly about anyone else's appearance either.
- Tell your child when she looks particularly nice – when she is dressed for a party, for example.
- If your child has a serious physical difficulty, make sure she understands what is wrong and teach her how to answer people's likely questions about it confidently. Ask your GP to refer you to a clinical psychologist if you need further advice.
- If your child has a serious birthmark, contact 'Let's Face It' or the 'Naevus Support Group' (addresses at the back of the book).

Personality

Children are born with different personalities but, to a certain extent, personality is also affected by experiences. Some children will be born with out-going personalities and they are more likely to be confident than children born with quiet, reserved personalities. However, quietness is not to be confused with a lack of confidence. Your child may prefer one or two good friends to being the life and soul of the party. Or she may enjoy her own company some of the time. This does not necessarily mean that she lacks confidence. Equally, a child who talks incessantly may lack confidence underneath. Accept your child's personality but recognise when she needs help with building confidence.

Parent tips

- Many parents who are themselves gregarious, want their children to be gregarious too. If your child is happy to be quiet, then accept this as part of her personality, but make sure that she is happy and not withdrawn or lacking in confidence.
- Look out for sudden changes in personality – this could indicate that confidence has been affected in some way.
- Do not give your child labels which make assumptions about her personality. For example, do not tell people in front of her that she is shy. She may then accept shyness as part of herself which will make it harder to overcome.
- Remember that you are trying to boost her confidence and not change her basic personality. After all, very few parents would ever want to change the basic make-up of their child.

Early experiences

Confidence can be knocked at any time. Even a confident adult can have his confidence damaged by one bad experience, although he is likely to pick himself up and get his confidence back fairly quickly. Children are more vulnerable and if their confidence is knocked, they may need your help to build it up again until it is stable enough to withstand life's inevitable ups and downs. Young children are naturally egocentric and will often see all problems as somehow their fault. The obvious example is when parents separate. Thinking it is their fault can make the experience even worse but reassurance by both parents can enable children to come through the experience with confidence intact. On a day-to-day basis, a child may refuse to try something again that she has failed at – perhaps she will not get back on her bike after a fall. But with her parents' help she can soon learn that she really can ride it and so get her confidence back immediately.

Parent tips

- Your child will be affected by bad experiences. Give the reassurance and encouragement needed, but be patient – telling your child to 'snap out of it' very rarely helps.
- Do not blame yourself if early experiences such as a long stay in hospital have affected your child badly. It is never too late to get confidence back again.
- Talk about what your child is experiencing at whatever level is appropriate for her age and allow her to talk about it too.
- Beware of being over-protective towards your child. She will sense your anxiety if something is wrong, so it may be better to be open with her.

The effect of parental style

This is something that parents obviously have most control over. However, you do not have to be a perfect parent to have confident children. In fact, parents aiming for perfection also tend to expect perfect children and there is clearly no such thing. Of course you will make mistakes and wish you had handled things differently and of course your children will go through phases when all their confidence seems to disappear.

Aiming to be some sort of super-parent often causes anxiety when you inevitably fall short of your ideal, and your child will sense this anxiety. It is probably best to accept that parenting is often an impossible task but to have a few clear aims for how you want to handle your children. To help foster confidence, it is best to allow children to be themselves and not what you want them to be, while offering clear guidelines of acceptable behaviour. Children who know what is expected of them tend to feel secure and security leads to confidence. Parents have an important role to play in encouraging children and praising their achievements. It is easy for a parent to feel proud of his child and just as easy to forget to tell her just how proud he feels. It is also easy to focus on your child's faults, trying to put them right while forgetting to tell her about her good points.

Parent tips

- Try to praise good behaviour and as far as possible ignore the bad.
- *Tell* your child when she has been helpful or done something well.
- Let your child overhear you telling someone else how proud you are of her achievements.
- Make sure you do not focus praise on just one aspect of your child's life such as academic achievement so that this becomes too important. Praise her for other things such as looking neat, being friendly or helpful or just for being good company.
- Your child should want to succeed for herself and not just to please you. Saying 'You must be very pleased' and 'I bet you feel good about that' helps focus on self-motivation too.
- Talk with your partner or anyone else involved with your child about ways of encouraging her. Building confidence should be a team effort.

The effect of school

Once your child starts school, she will suddenly seem to spend more time away from you and in the company of others. Hopefully, your child will start school confidently, helped by being well prepared for it. Teachers will note any children who are unsure and give them the reassurance and encouragement that they need. Part of their job is to ensure that children are motivated to work hard and succeed. If your child enjoys school then that motivation should come easily, but if your child does not then you will need to do something about it quickly. Of course, your child will need time to adjust if she is starting a new school or even going into a different class but if, after this settling in time, your child is clearly unhappy – perhaps not even wanting to go to school – then you need to take action. Talking to her teacher may uncover the cause of unhappiness – it may be something quite simple or something more serious such as bullying. Dealing with it quickly should help your child to get her confidence back.

There is nothing more likely to knock a child's confidence than failure, a fear of failure or a feeling of failure. If your child is struggling at school or feels different because she has a specific learning difficulty, then confidence can be affected badly. It is important to work with her teacher so that your child can achieve some success without comparing herself to more able children.

Parent tips

- If your child is finding the work difficult, ask for help as soon as possible. Ask if there is anything you can do at home and tell her teacher how it is affecting your child's confidence.
- Make sure that your child has some interests outside school that she can succeed in.

The effect of friends

If your child makes friends easily then she is likely to be confident in the company of other children. However, this is a chicken and egg situation because if your child is confident in the company of others, then she will make friends easily. Some children like to feel part of a group with lots of friends while others may be happy with just one close friend. Accept the sort of friendships that your child wants and always accept the friends that she chooses. Your child will fall out with friends and has to learn how to deal with that herself, although talking to you about it can help. A sympathetic ear is usually all that is needed rather than direct action. However, if your child seems to be making no friends at all, you may be able to offer practical help such as inviting round your friends who have children of the same age or encouraging your child to join a club. You cannot make friends for your child but you can create situations where she has to interact with other children.

Parent tips

- Never criticise your child's choice of friends – it is really criticising your child.
- Never compare your child to her friends with phrases such as 'Why can't you be more like Jennifer?'
- If you suspect bullying, go to the school straightaway. But remember that tiffs are part of growing up.
- If your child is secure in the knowledge that her family like her, then she will expect to be liked by other children.

Is it too late for your child?

It is obviously easier for parents who are reading this book when their child is just a young baby. They can think about parenting for confidence right from the start. But even for these parents, their child may turn out to have a shy personality and unexpected events could knock her confidence. The resulting low self-esteem or low self-confidence may be almost unavoidable. Many parents will be reading this book because their child lacks confidence already and that child may be a school child or even a teenager. Is it really too late for these children when it is clear that early experiences are so important?

The truth is, it's never too late although getting confidence back when it is low does not happen overnight. For most children, and indeed adults, confidence is not static anyway. Children can come through periods of low confidence relatively unscathed. The shyest, most withdrawn children can and do grow into confident adults. So it really is never too late and the starting point is for parents to have confidence in their own abilities to help their children grow into confident adults.

Checklist: HOW CONFIDENT IS YOUR CHILD?

1 You meet a friend in the street who asks your child what she has bought. Does your child:

a Look at your friend and answer directly?
b Answer your friend but by mumbling and looking down afterwards before she can ask anything else?
c Look to you for an answer?

2 You take your child to play with a new neighbour. Does your child:

a Look forward to it eagerly?
b Hang back when you get there and stay near you?
c Indicate that she does not want to go and cling to you on the way?

3 You go to buy your child some clothes. Does she:

a Tell you clearly which clothes she prefers?
b Wait for you to ask and then indicate a preference between two or three items?
c Let you do all the choosing?

4 You ask your child to take a card next door. Does she:

a Enjoy doing jobs like this?
b Enjoy doing it but with you or a brother or sister?
c Not enjoy jobs like this?

5 Another child grabs a toy off your child. Does she:

a Tell the other child what she thinks or grab it back?
b Run and tell you?
c Cry?

6 Your child has to perform a song with her class to the parents. Does she:

a Sing out loud and look ahead at the audience?
b Sing well when she practises at home but become overwhelmed on the occasion?
c Become upset on the occasion or not join in at all?

7 Does your child:

a Make new friends by taking the lead and going to talk to another child?
b Make new friends by responding to another child who approaches her?
c Find it difficult to make friends?

Imagine your child in the above situations. No child is completely predictable but thinking about how your child is likely to react can help you to consider what level of confidence she has. Mostly *a*s indicates a very confident child – but make sure that she is also sensitive to the needs of others. Mostly *b*s suggests that your child will be confident with help but that she still relies on your presence and reassurance before she demonstrates confident behaviour. This may be because of her age and she may need more experience of coping without you. Mostly *c*s suggests that your child needs a lot of positive parenting and encouragement to develop confidence – but, of course, she will get there in the end.

CHAPTER TWO

The shy child

A quiet child is not necessarily shy and a shy child is not necessarily quiet. Shyness is a difficulty relating to other people and a reluctance to make personal needs and wants known. As a result, shy children have poor social skills and find new situations difficult to cope with. While most shy children will be quiet and find communication difficult, particularly with unfamiliar people, others may be aggressive or loud.

Some children may be quietly confident. They can make their needs known and are not put off by unfamiliar situations or large groups of people. However, they are not gregarious and often prefer their own company. A parent who is very outgoing may wrongly think of her child as shy when he is quiet and happy to be so.

Why might your child be shy?

He was born that way. This may be partly true – we are all born with a predisposition to certain personality traits – but even children who seem to be shy right from the start can become more outgoing and assertive.

He has a shy parent. This can be an important factor. You are the role model for your child and he may sense your difficulties from a young age. He needs to see adults coping with social situations and talking to others confidently so that he can copy that pattern of behaviour.

He has low self-esteem. A child who does not think much of himself or his achievements may feel that he has little to offer others so he does not join in.

He has been told that he is shy. Most children will go through some clingy phases when they are adjusting to doing things without mum or dad. This may be when you go back to work or when he starts nursery. You may then label him as shy and so your child learns what is expected of him.

He has had a bad experience. Your child may have had a lot to cope with, whether from being in hospital or moving house a lot, or even losing someone close. This may result in your child avoiding social situations for a while. It may be more helpful to think of your child as going through an understandably shy 'patch' rather than think of him as a shy child.

He is going through a phase. Many children go through phases when shyness is more likely. This may be because of likely events at certain ages (starting nursery or school) or due to a stage of development (such as the stage of strong attachment at around nine months).

His shyness has been rewarded. Shyness at an early age can be rather cute. If your child gets the message that everyone goes 'Ahh, how sweet' when they see shy behaviour, then he may want to stay shy.

He is intelligent and artistic. Shyness does not automatically tie in with these attributes. Few children are happy to be shy, so beware of seeing shyness as something very positive and thus failing to help your child gain the confidence he needs.

Ten golden rules for dealing with your shy child

1 Accept your child's personality

You love your child as he is and do not want him to change, so tell him so. If you are outgoing and he is quiet and more introverted, then accept this and do not try to change his basic personality. Of course, if your child is shy and his shyness prevents him from enjoying life or even makes life difficult, then you will want to help make things easier for him. Make sure that he does not get the wrong message – that you wish he was a different child.

2 Understand child development

The following points on the key ages may help you to sort out the shy child from the one who is going through a shy phase.

- At nine months, babies develop a fear of strangers and some weeks later become very attached to you, which may result in clingyness.
- Between eighteen months and two-and-a-half years, children can become very clingy but will settle once you have left.
- Under threes will play alongside each other but very rarely together. They are egocentric and do not understand the needs of others well. They may hit and snatch to get what they want.
- Between the ages of three and five first friendships are formed, with children showing particular preferences for some friends. Children can now learn to cope in a group.
- At age four or five, your child will start school and should cope if he has been prepared well. Anxiety about new situations may manifest itself in clingy behaviour. If your child suddenly becomes shy or withdrawn during the school years, you should check with the school for academic difficulties or even bullying.
- During the teenage years, your child has to cope with changes in his body and emotions. Difficulty coping with these changes can result in shyness.

3 Understand your child's feelings

Just saying that you understand can help your child talk to you about his feelings. It can also help you talk to him. Maybe your child just does not want to go to a party, which may be difficult for you to understand – after all, he will have a good time when he gets there. It is all too easy to get angry and frustrated yourself and try to force him to go. You may even give him ultimatums – 'If you don't go, you won't get a party on your birthday.' He will soon learn that you don't understand and become even more introverted in the long term. Obviously, just before a party may not be the best time for a long chat about feeling shy, but you can indicate that you know how he feels while still being positive about going.

4 Be positive

It is important to feel positive about difficult events so that your child will respond to your optimism. Try to turn your child's negative thoughts into positive ones rather than just dismissing them as nonsense. For example, your child may express negative thoughts about social events by saying 'I don't want to go, no one likes me.' Do not just dismiss this with 'Don't be silly, of course people like you.' Show you understand and then add something positive, for example, you might say, 'I know how you feel but I happen to know that Geoff and Gavin like you' or 'Out of all the people at the party, someone will like you especially if you smile at them and chat to them.' Always give your child practical suggestions as well, so you might say, 'I know you won't know many people so why don't we offer a lift to Geoff so that you at least arrive with a friend.'

5 Do not label your child

Be careful about giving your child the label of being 'shy'. This is an easy trap to fall into and may just happen as you chat to friends saying, 'Of course, John is very shy.' You may even use it as an excuse when he doesn't answer or you may be comparing him with other children. Your child will then think of himself as shy, rather than someone who has just behaved in a shy way. Once a child gets a label, it can stick and everyone, including your child, expects shyness.

6 *Make it a team approach*

If you are the main carer, you may soon find strategies to deal with your child's shyness which work for him. For example, you may find that you can 'jolly' your child into a new situation. However, someone else dealing with your child may try a different strategy and one that, in the case of your child, is more likely to make matters worse. This may result in your child being even more clingy to you as other people clearly do not understand. Make sure that everyone your child deals with is aware of his shyness without feeling negative about it and that you talk to them about effective measures. Similarly, you may have done your best not to label him as shy in front of others only to find that everyone else is doing it! You may need to reply to someone's 'Isn't he shy' comment with something more positive such as 'Yes, John sometimes feels shy but he was really good and confident at the carol concert last week.'

7 *Let him know he's not alone*

Your child may feel different because everyone else seems to be joining in except him. It may help to talk about how everyone is different and about the different feelings we all have. Sometimes a story book about the subject can help younger children. You have to decide whether talking about shyness directly is appropriate for your child. For younger children this may just make it into a bigger issue than it is, but for older children who have recognised their shyness (and perhaps labelled themselves as shy), talking about it openly can help. It will show him that you understand and that you have time to listen.

8 *Watch and listen*

Be aware of what makes your child feel shy and note if there are any times when he can easily overcome his shyness. Some children have a particular skill or hobby which overrides shyness. For example, some very shy children are quite happy to sing a solo verse in front of everyone because they have experience of doing this well and easily. You can use these skills and situations to build your child's confidence.

9 *Praise your child*

This will come up again and again in this book. Shyness is a form of low confidence. It may be specific – a lack of confidence in a group or in new situations, for example. Praise your child whenever he copes well or just for being good company. You may say something like 'You did well going into Cubs on your own tonight – everyone certainly looked pleased to see you.' Or you might say 'Thank you for telling me all about school today – I love hearing about your interesting stories.'

10 *Make it easier for your child*

It may seem easier to make sure that your child just does not have to face difficult situations. He could stay at home with you, not join in with any group activities and not have any new situations to deal with. Of course, he may seem happy in the short term, although children who say they do not want to join in often do – it's just that they find it difficult. In the long term, your child will not be learning any social skills and will not learn to cope with new situations and consequently will become more shy. However, you can make it easier for your child by introducing him to new situations gradually or by being present for part of the time when he starts something new. Your aim will be that your child can join in independently but some children need to do this in smaller steps with guidance from you along the way. For many children, throwing them in at the deep end is not the ideal solution.

Making friends: how to help

Do not expect too much too young

Pre-school children are still learning about relating to other people and will go through a stage of playing alone or just alongside another child for at least the first three years. After this, they will still be very egocentric and fail to see the situation from another person's point of view.

A very young child may be aggressive and his limited language skills will add to his apparent need to snatch and grab. He will not have friends as such, just the companions which you have arranged for him. And these are very important so that he experiences other children. What you do and say is important too as he will be learning his social skills from you. So do expect a certain amount of anti-social behaviour such as snatching, but when you tell your child off make sure that you explain why so that he can learn to consider others. You may say 'Don't hit Jane or she will get hurt and cry. You don't like it when someone hits you, do you?' Or try 'If Jane has a turn first and then you have a turn, you will both be happy.' At first, your child will share and take turns to please you or avoid punishment but if you keep repeating the explanations, then he will develop his own moral reasons for co-operating.

Let your child choose his own friends

By criticising your child's friends, you are inadvertently criticising him. You may want your child to be friendly with your best friend's children – it's wonderful when it happens – but you cannot force friendships, so let your child decide. If your pre-school child cannot decide who to invite back to play, he may not have formed any firm friendships yet. Ask the playgroup leader who he seems to get on with.

A friend may behave badly in your home, especially a young child. Remember that this could have been your child in someone else's house, so do not be too harsh and ban them completely.

However, if a child consistently behaves badly and your child copies him, you may want to intervene. Talk to the other parent first. Tell your child how much you like his friends when he does choose someone appropriate.

Once a child starts school, he will sometimes seem to prefer the company of his friends to you. Remember not to be a clingy parent – he still needs you but he has other needs now, too.

Help your child to start a friendship

If your child seems ready to have friends but is always the child left on his own, you may need to help. Sometimes it is because your child finds a larger group of children difficult to handle. In this case, invite one child home from nursery, playgroup or school so that your child can get to know him in his own environment.

Your child may want to join in or start a conversation with another child but lacks the confidence to do so. Build your child's confidence in the way suggested in the rest of the book and at the same time offer him practical tips. You could start by acknowledging the problem, 'It's difficult to know what to say when you want to play with someone, isn't it?' Then make some suggestions such as 'Why don't you go and show Peter your new book?' You may even want to follow this up with some physical support, taking your child over to Peter and starting the conversation off for him. However, be careful that you do not force your child into a situation he is not ready for and never get cross if your child does not respond. By building up his confidence in other ways, your child will soon learn to make the first move.

Pre-school children are not like adults – they rarely go up to another child, introduce themselves and suggest that they play together. They have a much more non-verbal approach. The first move often involves going to play nearby without saying anything. Conversation follows once both children have watched the other and feel comfortable next to each other. So do not intervene too soon – give your child time to interact naturally.

Set an example

When someone new moves into the street or a new child starts at your child's school or playgroup, make sure your child sees and hears you going over and introducing yourself.

Be a friend to your child

A child's first friendship is usually with his mother. Make sure that you and your partner tell your child how much you like him and enjoy his company. Play with him and be a friend and he will learn that he can be good company and extend this outside the family. Encourage siblings to play together and do not reinforce sibling rivalry. While rivalry and squabbles are almost inevitable they can be exacerbated by comparing siblings ('Why can't you be like your sister?'). You can also encourage siblings to share and take turns in practical ways such as buying one large bag of crisps between them rather than two smaller ones.

Coping with new experiences: how to help

Prepare your child

Most children (and many adults) will have a fear of the unknown and will feel more comfortable if they know what to expect. Whenever your child is to experience something completely new or a major change in his life, make sure he knows exactly what is going to happen. Remember – what might be a fairly minor change to you, such as allowing your child to walk to school with friends instead of with you, may be a major change for your child. Also, do not assume that something is familiar to your child just because it is so familiar to you. Some parents forget that a first trip to the swimming pool or on a train can be an overwhelming experience for some children.

Preparing your child means talking about it – and usually not just once. Your child may not take some things in the first time you tell him, for instance, that you are going to move house. Talk about it several times and ask him questions to make sure that he fully understands. Talk about what, why, when and how. Tell him exactly what is going to happen in as much detail as he can understand and don't forget to tell him why. Time may be a difficult concept for pre-school children – 27 November means nothing. Try to give him some clues such as 'After your birthday but before we go on holiday.'

Take your child to see the new experience if possible. For example, make sure he visits his new nursery before officially starting. If your child is particularly unsure about, say, swimming you could visit the pool just to watch before trying it yourselves. You could also try telling stories and drawing pictures as part of your explanation. His play and pictures may tell you that he has not understood all the details. For example, one child played at moving house and his mother noticed that his lorries moved all the things back again after the move was finished. When she talked to him, she found that she had not made it clear that they would not be coming back again, except to visit.

Back off gently

While many children respond positively to being thrown in at the deep end, others do not. Whatever you do, you must stick to any promises so that if you said you would stay for as long as your child wanted, then you must stay. Gradual backing off is often a good compromise. You could stay at playgroup for most of the first session, just leaving for five minutes so that you child knows that part of the experience will be being left there. Gradually increase the time you stay away. *Check your own emotions* – your child will sense your own anxiety so try to feel and act confidently. Make sure that it is not you doing the clinging to your child!

Coping with groups: how to help

Some children are particularly shy when it comes to being part of a large group. All children have to get used to this if they are to cope with school, so how can you help?

Try to get your child used to the idea gradually, from an early age. Parent and toddler groups are ideal, where you go along with your child. Help your child to feel part of a smaller group by inviting small groups of friends round to play. If your child has difficulty later on, liaise with the nursery, playgroup or school so that they understand this part of your child's shyness. They may give your child some responsibility so that he feels an important part of the group.

Similarly, parties can present a no-win situation for shy children. Joining in can be too hard and yet not joining in is hard too. See if your child can arrive early and help with some of the organisation. Or arrange to have one friend round first so that they can settle in together at home and then travel and arrive at the party together.

Above all, *understand.* Try to see all group situations from your shy child's point of view. How must he be feeling and how can you help? Tell him that you understand how he feels.

Shyness with speaking: how to help

First of all, don't force it. Never force your child to speak with comments like 'Go on, speak to Auntie Jane then' or even 'Speak when you are spoken to!' They rarely help and just serve to make your child more self-conscious. Encourage your child to speak while giving him the opportunity not to. You might say 'We went swimming yesterday, didn't we Sam?' and then leave a pause in case he wants to contribute. If you sense that your child may participate in the conversation, you might give him a lead in, such as 'Tell Auntie Jane how you jumped off the diving board.'

Try to keep your child involved. Do not exclude him from conversations completely by not expecting him to say anything at all. He will soon learn that nothing is expected from him. Instead use some lead-in comments and encourage any participation even if it is non-verbal such as a nod of the head. Try also not to put him off. Do not expect a young child to have all the 'niceties' of speech. While not wanting to encourage interruptions you may want to make allowances for a shy child. It would be a shame to put a child off his few efforts with endless nags like 'Don't interrupt' or even 'Wait until you are spoken to!' Make sure you show an interest in everything your child says to you by giving him your full attention whenever possible. You can even tell him that he is interesting to talk to.

Older children may respond to very direct role playing. Talk about how difficult it is to speak to people in specific situations, whether it's asking for something in a shop or talking to a teacher. Now act it out together. With younger children you can be less direct but even playing at shops or cafes can help.

The shy parent

If you were shy as a child or are still shy now, this will understandably have an effect on the way you deal with your shy child. You may have bad memories of being a shy child and therefore be very anxious in case your own child has the same experiences. This can result in you over-reacting to your child's shyness or else your child may sense your anxiety. Talk to your partner about it or even someone less emotionally involved so that you can make sure that you do not over-react.

You may blame yourself for your child's shyness, either because you think he has inherited it or because you feel he is copying your current shyness. Guilt is very destructive and can be picked up by your child. An older child may even use your guilt and blame you for his own difficulties. Guilt leads to anxiety which is not conducive to positive parenting. You need to be positive that your child can overcome his shyness and show positive and confident behaviour yourself.

If you are shy, you may want to tackle your shyness or lack of confidence at the same time. Enrol for an assertiveness course or make yourself face situations which are difficult for you such as joining a new club. Do make sure, however, that you are not seeing a problem where there is none. Parents who were shy children themselves are more likely to look out for shyness in their own children. If your child is quietly confident, then there may be little cause for concern.

Parents say . . .

'The only way I could get Gemma to join in at parties was by bribery or threat. I would stay with her and if she didn't play the game I would tell her that she wouldn't get a party bag at the end. Then I realised what pressure I was putting her under. I got my husband to take her to parties and he would leave her there even if she objected. We were always told that once he left she settled in and played the games, albeit very quietly. I think we made too much of her shyness. Once we relaxed, so did she.'

(Mother of Gemma, 6)

'Another mother with a child at playgroup told me what a nice girl Camilla was. She had a very noisy and rather bossy daughter who would go up to anyone and give her opinion! For the first time I realised that being quiet or even shy is not such a bad thing.'

(Mother of Camilla, 3)

'We sent James to a Montessori nursery who have a philosophy of looking at the whole child. They

tackled his shyness right from the start by giving him lots of jobs to do so he felt important. Within a few weeks, he was even taking messages around the nursery. We took this up at home and gave him some responsibility with his own little jobs. It worked wonders.'

(Father of James, 4)

'Becky has been shy as long as I can remember but it got rather worse when secondary school approached. I managed to get together with some other people who already had children at the big school. When Becky met them, I encouraged her to ask them about it. Luckily they liked it there and their attitude seemed to rub off on Becky. I'm sure it helped to know all the little details about secondary school life that you don't really pick up at the official visit.'

(Mother of Rebecca, 11)

Checklist: IS YOUR CHILD SHY?

1 You take your child to the pantomime. Volunteers are asked to go up onto the stage. Does he:

a Put his hand up but back out when he is chosen?
b Never volunteer, preferring to watch the other children go up?
c Go up on stage eagerly?

2 New neighbours move in next door. You take your child to meet them. Is he:

a Hiding behind you before you even get there?
b Pleased to come with you but unlikely to speak at all?
c Eager to meet them?

3 Your child is chosen to play a part in the nativity play at school. There will be lots of rehearsals and then a performance to the parents.

a Do you worry that on the day your child will refuse to take part?
b Will your child be reluctant at first but once he knows what he is expected to do, relax into the part well?
c Will he love the rehearsals and the performance?

4 A new club is started up and members are being sought. Will your child:

a Ask to join spontaneously but feel a bit frightened or nervous on the day?
b Never ask to join anything like that at all?
c Be a keen member right from the start?

5 You have taught your child to answer the telephone appropriately. When it rings, does he:

a Rush to answer it but not feel sure what to say when he picks it up?
b Ignore it and wait for you to answer it?
c Answer it confidently?

There are no right and wrong answers to these questions and in fact your child may respond in a completely different way to the options here. But by thinking about how your child might respond in these situations you can decide if he is shy, lacking in confidence or just more introverted than some other children.

If you answered *a* to questions 1, 4 and 5, it may be that your child wants to be outgoing but lacks that last bit of confidence. However, if you answered *b* to questions 1 and 2, then perhaps your child is happy to be quiet and watch. Thinking about the situation in question 3 may indicate that your child's shyness is linked to a fear of the unknown and that preparing him in advance will help. When you consider question 5, think about other situations which your child may cope with well. Many shy children are very good on the telephone, for example, and this could be used to boost confidence in other areas.

CHAPTER THREE

Parenting for confidence

For your child to be confident, you need to be confident yourself. In particular, you need to be confident in your own parenting skills. If you are shy or lack assertiveness, you may want to tackle this at the same time as helping your child with the same problems. Some ideas for shy parents were given in Chapter 2 and for older children you can be quite direct about this, creating a sense of 'going through it' together. In fact, if your child is in some way giving *you* help and encouragement as well, this can in itself help her own confidence.

How we respond to our children will obviously affect their confidence and self-esteem. Although there are many factors affecting your child's confidence, from specific experiences to the personality she was born with, there is no doubt that parental handling has an important impact. Of course, building your child's confidence from an early age can prevent problems occurring, but it is never too late to think about parenting skills as a way of boosting confidence in a child who lacks it.

1 Don't try to be a super-parent

To be confident about parenting skills is hard for any parent, even those who are super-confident in other areas of life. All parents have one thing in common – they are thrown in at the deep end and have to learn as they go along, sometimes, inevitably, by their mistakes. There are no qualifications to be taken in parenting and the advice we receive as new parents is often confusing and conflicting. And because good parenting is so important to us, we set very high, often impossible, standards.

Be realistic

There is no such thing as a perfect parent and there is no such thing as a perfect child. This seems obvious and yet, when it comes to parenting we expect to be faultless and if our children are anything but perfect, we blame ourselves. Setting unrealistic goals inevitably leads to guilt when we fall short of our expectations.

Be realistic – there are times when all parents will be tired or unwell and therefore not as patient as they might wish to be. Look on this positively – it is important for children of all ages to realise that parents are human too. They need to learn that mum and dad have feelings and emotions. Tell your child when you are not feeling up to a romp on the floor or having a friend to play. And explain why. Eventually, they will understand.

Don't feel guilty

Many parents feel guilty if they are not helping with homework, being understanding about an argument with a friend, making something out of an empty egg box and a toilet roll and playing some frightfully educational game all at the same time. Not only do you need time and space to yourself but so do the children. Parenting may feel like a twenty-eight-hour-a-day job but you do need time off. Use your partner, Grandma, neighbour or friend to ease the burden. And remember that you are helping with your child's confidence if she has to rely on different people or be more independent occasionally.

Don't blame yourself

Your child will not be perfect all the time and it is not your fault. All toddlers go through stages of having temper tantrums, all school children have arguments with friends and all teenagers will be moody on occasions. So don't blame yourself. The same applies to children who lack confidence. All parents can look back and identify situations which they could have handled differently but a lack of confidence is usually the result of many factors. Look at the parenting skills you need now rather than looking back with guilt. Even then, you won't get it right all the time. You can only have overall strategies for dealing with your children's problems – occasional lapses or mistakes are inevitable. Tell your child if you have made a mistake – 'Sorry, I shouldn't have said that' or 'I didn't realise that you would find that difficult, next time I'll come with you.'

2 Seek expert help – but don't forget your own abilities

Most of the advice you receive about bringing up your child will not have been asked for. Advice on how to deal with a shy child or one lacking in confidence will be just as forthcoming. Not all of it will be helpful but if you are very concerned about your child you can find yourself believing everyone and everything.

Is the advice based on experience?

Listening to parents of other children can be helpful. It is certainly reassuring to know just how common the problem is, and if you can exchange practical ideas which may help, so much the better. However, every child is different and you will need to take the advice which is applicable to your child and her situation. It is most helpful to talk with other parents who have a positive view of building a child's confidence. Inevitably, you will meet parents who have labelled their child as shy or lacking in confidence and who see this as totally negative and very long term.

What about expert advice?

You may decide to seek expert help with your child's lack of confidence and this is dealt with in Chapter 9. It may be that you want to talk it through with an expert yourself before involving your child directly. In fact, you may not want your child to be involved with the expert at all. This can be very helpful as you will be speaking to someone, whether it is your health visitor or a clinical psychologist, who will have experience of many families with similar problems. It is likely to be reassuring and helpful to talk to someone outside the family who is not emotionally involved.

Your own expertise

Always remember that you are the real expert on your child, although an outsider can help you to view the situation more objectively. You know what is likely to work for your child and how to handle certain situations. Have confidence in your own abilities as a parent and talk over strategies for building your child's confidence with your partner and other people closely involved with your child.

Bus-stop advice

You will inevitably receive advice from passing acquaintances who mean well but do not really know your child. When you are desperate, it is easy to take this advice to heart even though it may be inappropriate. Strangers have been known to mutter unhelpful advice such as 'What that child needs is a good smack' or 'Children should be made to answer their elders.' Ignore this 'advice' and seek help from an expert or caring friend.

3 Consider the whole family

Each child's confidence is affected by the other members of the family. A child lacking in confidence has different needs from a child who is super-confident and it is not unusual for both types of children to exist in the same family.

Try to balance your time. This does not mean that you have to spend an equal amount of time with each child each day. That would be impossible and is not always for the best. While you will want to have some time on your own with each child occasionally, there are bound to be times when one child needs a bit of extra attention from you. However, always be aware of the needs of each child. The quiet, well-behaved child is easy to ignore while the child going through a difficult phase or having problems may be getting all your time and attention. Make sure that no child sees that 'being a problem' can be rewarding.

Ensure that each child experiences success

Being successful or good at something can boost anyone's confidence. But what if one child is experiencing success but not her brother or sister? Sometimes a lack of confidence can come from being overshadowed by a sibling who has a particular talent or is particularly successful at school. The achievements of the successful child get a great deal of attention, while the other child may be comparing herself unfavourably. Try to avoid competition between siblings by encouraging them to have different interests. Make sure that each child is successful at something and do not put too great a value on one type of achievement. For example, it is easy to praise one child for her success at school if this is important to you, while ignoring the less able child's ability to draw or sing. Never compare siblings or set any sort of competition between them which might cause jealousy or frustration.

4 Take the lead from your child

It is important to go at your child's pace. It may be that your child is uncertain of new situations to start with but given time can cope well. Forcing your child into a situation which she is not yet ready for can actually hold her back. Although you will need to let your child set the pace, she will also need gentle encouragement to move forward and gain confidence in more and more situations.

Focus on confident phases

Some children will go through life quite confidently until they hit a 'sticky patch' and will then seem to lose all their confidence very suddenly. Children who are inconsistent in this way can be difficult to deal with as you never know what to expect and how they are going to react. Instead of worrying about the times of low confidence, concentrate on the confident moments. Praise your child whenever she shows confident behaviour and set new challenges when she seems to be in the right frame of mind to deal with them. So, if she is reluctant to, say, join a new club one week, you could ask again when she has just shown confidence with something else. In other words, build on the confidence she has and try to extend confident phases so the shy phases come less frequently.

Listen to your child

It is important that your child can talk about her problems so that she can start to tackle them herself. Even a very young child may tell you that she feels shy or finds something difficult. However, children of all ages may not be very direct when they mention confidence and it is up to you to pick up the clues – both verbal and non-verbal. To start with, your child will need someone who will listen and understand. The practical help comes after this.

5 Set boundaries but encourage independence

Children need to know what is expected of them by having clear rules and boundaries. Obviously pre-school children will learn what is acceptable behaviour as they grow and there should be as few grey areas as possible. It is no good deciding that your child should not be allowed to eat sweets before dinner but then give in one day because you are feeling tired and do not feel like an argument or tantrum. You will occasionally need to be flexible – perhaps a poorly child can watch more television than is normally allowed – but always give reasons for stretching the rules.

Let your child decide the rules

Once your child is at school, and certainly once she is a teenager, you can agree some rules together. Explain that rules are necessary as a way of considering everyone else in the house. Your child may want some rules of her own, such as people knocking before going into her room. Take her views into consideration as this will help her self-esteem as well as her skills of independence.

Encourage independence

If your child is to grow into a confident adult then she will gradually need to be given more and more independence. From an early age, her views should be taken seriously and listened to. Even a very young child may have an opinion on where you go for a picnic or where you should go for your family holiday. Allow your child to make some of her own choices such as what she wears each day, and as she matures allow her as much independence as she can cope with. Show your child that you trust her while setting realistic boundaries. For example, you may allow your child to walk down the road to a friend's house provided she comes back at a stated time. If you are unsure of this, it may be better to watch from the window rather than walk her all the way there every time. Your child will then have a feeling of being able to cope on her own even though you have discretely kept an eye on things.

6 Praise your child

Praising your child and telling her how proud you are of her is the easiest and most effective way of building her confidence. We all like to be told we have done well and that we are nice to be with, and children are no exception. However, at the same time you will want your child to feel proud of herself so that she does not just achieve things to please you.

Do not just praise your child for academic achievements and nothing else. Using praise for just one small area of your child's life can actually put pressure on her to succeed at that while making other areas of achievement seem unimportant. Praise your child for being kind to a brother or sister, for helping you at home, for thinking about other people, for finishing her meal or for crossing the road sensibly. The list is endless. Of course, you will not want to overdo it or the praise can lose its meaning, but praise where it's due will give your child the confidence she deserves.

Tell your child what you like about her, again making sure that you do not focus on just one thing, such as her physical appearance. A child who is constantly told what pretty hair she has but not praised for any other personal attributes may learn that physical appearance is what counts. Yes, tell her when she looks nice but tell her when she's *being* nice as well. Tell her when she is kind, thoughtful or just good company. Make sure that your child likes herself as this is the essence of confidence. However, you will want to ensure that she is aware of other people's good points too. Too much praise can leave a child with a sense of too much self-importance. This can be helped by praising your child for thinking of other people and by openly praising others too.

Try to make your praise specific. Give your child real examples of what you like about her. You might say 'I liked the way you helped your friend when she fell over' or 'I was very proud of the way you played so well with your younger sister today.'

Lastly, let your child know what *she does for you*. Your child will be aware that she takes up your time when you are busy, that she costs money and that she creates problems and arguments. But does she realise what a positive addition she has been to your life? We may never stop to tell our children that we are so glad that we had them, that they are worth any hassles and that life would not have been as happy without them. Similarly, we just assume our children know that we love them without having to say it. Say 'I love you' and tell your child what she has brought to your life.

The great punishment debate

Should you punish your child and if so, should that punishment be physical? Many parents will have very strong views on this which may be based on their own experiences as children. It is important to consider punishment together with reward and praise. Punishing bad behaviour while ignoring the good will undoubtedly result in more bad behaviour – after all this is how the child is getting attention. It is also important to consider punishment in relation to your child's confidence. Setting clear boundaries can help with confidence but too much punishment can undermine confidence, leaving your child with a feeling of not getting anything right. For your child to feel confident, she needs to like herself. And in order to like herself she must get feedback from others that she is a likeable person. So, even when punishment is necessary, it is important to be clear that it is what your child did that you do not like and not the child herself.

Ignoring bad behaviour

This has to be accompanied by praising good behaviour. This works very well indeed for most situations. For example, buy a treat for a child who has sat quietly in the supermarket trolley and tell her why. Ignore a child who is having a shopping-time tantrum, perhaps demanding sweets. She is not doing any harm screaming in her trolley nor is she getting any attention. However, once she has calmed down, you can then reward her with a hug and tell her why she behaved badly. Some bad behaviour cannot be ignored but can nevertheless be dealt with quickly and calmly, such as taking the paint away from a child who has painted the kitchen wall. Giving explanations ensures that your child's confidence is not affected – she will know that you like her from all your praise at other times but it will be clear that her behaviour is unacceptable.

Smacking

This is immediate and can stop bad behaviour instantly. However, you are showing your child that problems can be solved with aggression so, in the long term, she is more likely to be aggressive herself. Always explain why you have smacked your child and if you did it out of temper, do not be afraid to apologise. A child who is smacked but does not know why will lose confidence and self-esteem very quickly.

Time out

This can also be immediate – you simply remove your child from the situation to a place on her own. For example, a child misbehaving at the meal table can be put on a chair in the hall until she apologises or for a certain amount of time. However, remember that ten minutes is a long time for a pre-school child. Also, it may not be appropriate to send a young child to her bedroom as she will start to have negative views of this room which can affect sleeping patterns. Once your child is allowed back with the rest of the family, you can tell her how welcome her company is now that she is behaving well. This will ensure that your child has got the message about her behaviour being unacceptable while still allowing her to retain her self-esteem.

Withdrawal of privileges

This is often most appropriate for older children and can include 'grounding' your child for as long as necessary. However, it is important for your child to understand why a privilege has been withdrawn and for older children to agree to some basic rules of behaviour first. Withdrawing a privilege need not affect confidence, but do listen to your child's point of view as she moves into the school years and particularly the teenage years.

Shouting

This is often punishment enough for a pre-school child who is still eager to please you. However, do remember that the more often you shout, the less impact it will have. Shouting in response to bad behaviour should not, in itself, affect confidence, but beware of what you shout out in temper. 'Get out of my sight' can make a child feel that you really don't like her and takes the focus off the behaviour and onto her. 'Why can't you be like . . .' is also easy to shout out in temper and frustration and inevitably knocks confidence.

Dos and don'ts of punishment

Do make sure that your child is praised more than she is punished. If your child is playing nicely while you get on with your ironing, tell her how good she's being.

Don't wait until your child does something wrong before she gets your attention.

Do use rewards. Buy her a comic for being good while you shop.

Do tell your child that you like her. You can even do this at the same time as telling her off by saying something like, 'I was very disappointed when you hit your friend because normally you are very nice to be with.'

Do show that you have confidence that your child won't do it again. You might say something like 'I know you won't hit your friend again because you don't really want to hurt him and next time you will tell me if there is a problem with sharing the toys.'

Don't use threats which you do not intend to carry out. Your child will feel more secure and therefore confident if she knows what to expect. If you say 'If you do that again we will not go to the park' stick to it.

Do be flexible, on the other hand. Children should be given some credit for apologising or owning up. Your child will gain confidence if she feels that she can sometimes put things right herself.
Don't ever threaten your child with loss of love. Never tell your child you don't like her or won't like her any more if she does something wrong again. To like herself, she has to be totally confident that you like her, whatever happens.

The things parents say . . .

Of course we will need to tell our children when their behaviour is unacceptable and of course we will need to lay down some rules and guidelines. However, there are ways of saying these things so that confidence remains intact. Sometimes, what we say is unnecessary and unhelpful and may have just been said out of temper without considering the effect it is having on our children. It is worth thinking about what you say and how you say it.

'You always do that' is very negative and implies that your child just cannot get it right and is unlikely to do so in the future. Far better to say 'You've done that before, now how can we put it right?'

'You're so forgetful' is labelling your child and, again, implies that nothing will change. Just reprimand your child for the one incident of forgetfulness and talk about how to remember in the future.

'When I was your age' implies that you were a much better child which is probably not true. It is better to look back on your own childhood as a way of understanding how hard it can be – 'I remember finding it hard to make new friends when I was eleven.'

Look what you've made me do now' lets your child take the blame for everything. Allowing your child to feel responsible for everything that goes wrong in the family will really lower her self-esteem.

'I suppose you think that's clever' is one of the many things our parents said to us and we catch ourselves saying to our own children. What does it mean? At best it is a piece of sarcasm – a put-down which your child can do without.

'Grow up' is another piece of vagueness. If your child is behaving in an immature way, try to find out why and help to put it right. No child knows what you expect her to do when you tell her to grow up or pull herself together.

Write down all the negative put-downs that you use and think about how to make them more positive. Of course, you want to let your child know what she has done wrong, but have you given her some suggestions as to how she might put it right? And have you indicated that you are confident that she can get it right next time?

The things parents do . . .

Make assumptions about what a child likes

You may even go as far as to say 'When she grows up, she's bound to work with children – she loves little ones.' Children need to decide what their own likes and dislikes are and to be able to express them. It is essential for a child's self-esteem to know that her views are important and that she does not have to like the same things as you.

Forget to watch as well as listen

Listening to your child is so important, but sometimes you need to pick up non-verbal clues to understand what she is trying to tell you. Even a child's bad behaviour can be telling you that something is wrong. Parents need to watch their own non-verbal signals too. A sarcastic smile or a shake of the head to show how wronged you are can be a put-down on its own.

Check everything a child does

You must show you trust your child completely and this means not hovering about when you have delegated a task to her. For example, you may decide that your child is now able to get her own lunch box ready for school. Trust her to do it and do not check the contents unless you have agreed to do this on the first occasion. If your child forgets her drink – then she'll remember it the next day and no harm has been done. Meanwhile, you have shown that you trust her and this helps her confidence.

Fail to stand up for their children

There will be times when your child needs someone in her corner. Perhaps she is being bullied at school or perhaps she has been treated badly by an adult in authority. Show that you understand and are prepared to speak up on her behalf – if that is what she wants. If she comes to you with a problem which you dismiss as unimportant or do not quite believe, then she will give up on you. Meanwhile, the situation could adversely affect her confidence while you missed the opportunity to listen and perhaps act before it got out of hand.

Put their own values on a child's achievements

Try to put yourself on your child's level when it comes to praising her achievements. Your child may be very proud of something she has made out of an egg box and empty toilet roll. Join in with her pleasure and show her how pleased you are too, even if you thought the painting last week was much better. Your child must gradually learn to do things which she can be pleased with for herself and not just aim to please you. Self-confidence comes from knowing that what you do and say is worthwhile without anyone telling you. So reinforce your child's own pride in her achievements.

Parents say . . .

All parents feel guilty. The only way to handle it is to laugh at yourself. And get together with other parents and all laugh together. It's all too easy to forget that being a parent can be fun and rewarding. Since I 'lightened up' as my son would say, so have the children.

(Mother of Tom, 8 and Hannah, 6)

Having two or three children helps. We all panic when our first child has tantrums or threatens to leave home or tells you what an awful mother you are – next time round, you take it all in your stride.

(Mother of three children aged 5, 11 and 13)

The worst thing for me was coming home to find Camilla playing up. The last thing you want to do when you haven't seen her all day is shout or tell her off – you feel so guilty. But I realise now that she tests me out so I give her a short, sharp reprimand and then make up by having a story and a cuddle together.

(Mother of Camilla, 3)

I think you find what works best for each child – probably by trial and error. Sarah gets distraught if you tell her off and then feels desperately sorry. Jack needs much firmer handling – I usually stop him playing out with his friends when he misbehaves.

(Mother of Jack, 9 and Sarah, 4)

Checklist: ARE YOU A CONFIDENT PARENT?

- When did you last tell your child that you liked being with her?
- When did you last ask for your child's views when making a family decision?
- Think of two things you praised your child for last week. Did you use more than two put-downs?
- Can you think of five things your child is particularly good at? Does your child know that she is good at them?
- Do you ever do something for your child because it is quicker and easier when she could easily have managed herself?
- Are you prepared to apologise to your child if necessary?
- Can you still feel proud of your child if she has chosen to go out in scruffy ill-matching clothes?
- Do you know which times of the day your child is most likely to want to talk to you?
- Do you ever buy your child things out of guilt?
- Are you happy to be a good parent most of the time or are you still trying to be that perfect all-things-to-all-people parent?

CHAPTER FOUR

When confidence is challenged

All parents want their children to have a happy, carefree childhood devoid of worries and problems. Some may even go so far as to protect their children from worries by not being open about difficult events. Some parents may have had unhappy childhoods themselves and set out determined that their children will have nothing but happiness.

The perfect childhood does not exist, of course. And while we would not wish any major problems on our children, we should accept that children will have to deal with, at the very least, minor problems at school and with friendships. Others will have divorce, changes such as moving away from friends and even bereavement to contend with. We cannot always protect our children from problems and should not be too negative when they occur. Children have a lot to learn from coping with difficult events – it certainly prepares them for the inevitable problems and challenges of adulthood.

In fact, if a child really is having a totally carefree childhood with twenty-four hours a day happiness, the chances are that he is being overprotected by parents. Children must learn how to cope with the ups and downs of life and parents can help them do this.

Changes and difficult situations can always affect your child's confidence, although this will depend on how situations are handled as well as the personality of your child. Some children even have differences to cope with right from the start – perhaps they look different or come from unusual family backgrounds. It is important to be aware of the situations which can knock a child's confidence and think about the best way of handling them when they do occur. And if you feel your child's confidence has already been knocked by life events, it may be worth looking back at what affected your child as well as forward in your efforts to re-build the confidence which was there before.

Coping with changes

Tell your child at the right time

Your child will need time to come to terms with any imminent change and you will need time to prepare him for it. However, you will not want to talk about it too far ahead so that anxiety has time to build up. Remember, pre-school children have a limited idea of time and telling them that a baby is due in eight months or that they are starting school in a year is fairly meaningless to them. After a few weeks of nothing happening, they will soon lose interest and when the time comes will hardly believe it is happening. Decide on a good time to tell your child and help a younger child to get a sense of the time-scale involved with a chart or calendar.

Be positive yourself

When a change is about to occur, you must be positive yourself and point out all the advantages. For example, if you are to move house, show your child that it is a good thing by talking about all the positive aspects of the place you are going to. Get as much information as you can so that you can reassure him that there is a swimming pool nearby or another Cub pack he can join. At the same time feel positive that your child will cope with the change and even benefit from it – your child will sense any negative feelings that you have.

Acknowledge your child's feelings

Although you will want to create a positive picture of the change, you must acknowledge your child's reservations about it and listen to his concerns. Make practical suggestions to help. For example, if your child is changing schools and is worried about losing friends, reassure him that old friends can still come to play and give him an address/telephone book so that he can contact them easily once he is no longer seeing them at school. However, at the same time you can be positive about the future, reassuring him that new friends will be made.

Keep listening and talking

Your child will not take everything in at once when you explain about the change, whatever his age. Let your child take the lead and drop everything to answer any questions as they arise. Sometimes a book can help open up the lines of communication particularly with a young child. There are stories about most of the main changes your child is likely to experience, including starting school, coping with parents' separation, moving house and having a new baby. Ask your librarian to help you find an appropriate book for the age of your child.

Do not make assumptions

Do not assume that your child understands the obvious. Why should a very young child know that when you move house you don't move back again the next year? And why should a young child know the meanings of words like 'separation' or 'divorce'. Explain everything in at least two different ways, using simple language, and ask questions to make sure that your child has understood.

Do not assume that your child feels as you do. You may feel very happy about a change but that does not mean that your child does. Or you may be apprehensive while your child takes it all in his stride.

Be prepared for changing emotions

Your child may seem to be very happy about an imminent change and even be looking forward to it. However, the reality may not match his expectations so be prepared for a change of heart. For example, your child may be looking forward very positively to a new baby brother or sister. However, when the baby arrives your child may have to cope with jealous feelings which you could not really prepare him for. He may not be prepared for a change in his feelings but you should be.

Keep your support going

Different children take different lengths of time to adapt to a change. Some children seem to adapt straightaway but there can be a delayed reaction. This may be triggered by a particular event such as Christmas after parents have separated or the date of the local pet show after a dog has died. The reason for a sudden upset or bout of bad behaviour may not always be obvious, but if there has been a major change in your child's life during the last year, this should always be considered and your child given the opportunity to discuss it once more.

Top confidence knockers

1 Parents' divorce or separation

The reason that this can knock a child's confidence so much is that all children are at risk of blaming themselves. Some children will even name particular situations, involving themselves, which they think caused the separation. Many children will try to get their parents back together again and then feel a failure when they do not succeed.

The other effect on a child's confidence is the sudden focus on other things. Children can feel ignored and even unwanted while parents battle over what is left of their marriage. Parents will understandably feel sad, depressed and even rather negative about the future. This rubs off on children who also start to feel negative. However, confidence in children can be retained if both parents make the children a priority and are aware of the effect the change is having on them.

- However hard, tell the children about the separation together.
- Actually say that it is not their fault and that you both still love them as much as ever.
- Give your children extra attention during this difficult time.
- Make sure that the changes come gradually. If one parent moves out then this is enough to cope with so keep to the usual routine as far as possible.
- Let your children talk to other children in the same situation, carefully choosing families that have coped well.
- Seek expert help early on and take more detailed advice on how to help the children. Some conciliation centres will also counsel children.

2 Bereavement

Coming to terms with a death can also knock a child's confidence. This is because he will have very strong emotions to deal with and this can be frightening. Like adults, some children may even blame themselves for a death and this will have a strong effect too.

- Allow your child to grieve any death; even the death of a goldfish can be devastating to a young child.
- If the whole family is grieving, it is easy to forget a child who may outwardly seem to be coping well. Check that your child

has understood exactly what has happened and talk openly about the dead person.

- Talk to a bereavement counsellor (CRUSE – address at the back of the book).
- The counsellor or a book on bereavement can help you to understand as much as you can about the process of bereavement, including the stages of denial, anger and sadness. Your child will go through similar stages.
- You will want to work towards your child accepting what has happened and having a positive view of the future. You will need to have a positive view yourself in order to help him towards this.

3 Moving house

This can affect your child's confidence, particularly if you are moving to a different part of the country. This is because your child can feel insecure among unfamiliar places and people. There is always a fear of the unknown, together with a sadness at leaving a familiar and friendly environment.

- Make sure your child knows as much as possible about the new area. Take a picture of the new house before you move so that he can start visualising himself there.
- If there is something that will help your child feel positive about the move, such as a big tree to climb in the garden, take a picture of this too.
- Talk about exactly what will happen on the day of the move and afterwards. Ask your child questions to ensure he has understood.
- Prepare a new routine in advance so that your child can start at toddler group, swimming or drama club etc. as soon as possible.
- When you move, sort your child's bedroom out first as this can help him feel secure again.

4 Sudden failure

Of course, failure may not be sudden and this can affect confidence just as much. For example, school failure is dealt with in detail in Chapter 7 together with bullying, which can also adversely affect confidence.

A feeling of failure can occur at any time and the key word here is *feeling* – your child may not have failed at all but as long as he feels that he has failed then low confidence will result.

- Find at least one thing which your child can succeed at and praise your child's success. An overall feeling of success will help him cope with occasional 'failures'.
- Success does not have to mean being better than other people at a chosen activity. Perhaps your child could do something non-competitive which cannot be compared with the rest of the family. This could be anything from growing vegetables to decorating the kitchen wall with his pictures.
- Your child cannot expect to be good at everything but a highly competitive child will feel that he has failed if he is anything but the best. Make sure you praise your child for just taking part or trying and do not put too high a value on being the best or winning.
- Teach your child to cope with failure and losing from an early age. Play family games together and model being a good loser. Do not make a big thing of winning but tell your child what fun it is to play together.
- Acknowledge your child's disappointment when he does experience failure but give him practical ideas for doing better next time. Always remind your child of his strengths.

5 Other problems

Of course, anything can happen to knock your child's confidence suddenly – the list is endless. Your role as a parent is to recognise when confidence has been affected and then help your child to 'bounce back' as quickly as possible.

- Help your child to tackle a problem head on. Do not solve all his problems for him or brush them aside as unimportant.
- Help your child to get through difficult periods – such as exam time – by organising something to look forward to afterwards.
- Encourage your child to see something positive in what at first seems to be a failure or problem. Recognise that your child is learning through mistakes and through tackling problems.
- Make sure you spot the times when your child needs that extra bit of encouragement and support.
- Encourage your child to talk it through with you. If your child already knows he could have done better, then it may not be necessary or even helpful to keep telling him.

Coping with outside pressures

Your child will start by learning to be confident in familiar surroundings with people who know and love him. Gradually, the outside world has more influence and you seem to have less. By the time your child starts school, you cannot protect him from outside pressures but you can help him to cope.

Pressure from the media

This is most applicable to older children watching television. Your child may want to be like a television idol either in achievements or looks and feel he has failed by not living up to the image. Adverts may persuade your child that he needs to be thinner/fitter, have shinier hair or own the latest toy or computer.

- Work on your child's self-esteem in all areas. If you tell him he looks nice and has certain attractive features, he will be less inclined to try to model himself on someone else. This can be particularly true of girls, who feel the need to be super thin like all the models.
- If watching television is central to your child's life, then it is

more likely to influence him. Talk to him about limiting viewing time and being selective about what programmes to watch.

- Talk openly about adverts to an older child, getting him to see how they are trying to sell the product. Laughing about them together can sometimes help.
- Be aware that the media can also put over a very negative view of life, with features on unemployment and ill-health dominating the news at times. Your child needs to be optimistic about his future so don't make assumptions that failure is inevitable because of the state of society.
- Encourage your child to choose magazines suitable for his age group. Younger children choosing teen magazines may feel pressure to look or behave in a way inappropriate for their age.

Pressure from peers

Your child needs enough confidence to be the one that says 'No' when a group of children are persuading him to say 'Yes'. It takes a confident child to wear something different from the crowd, to tell his peers that they are wrong and to have some of his own goals which have not been influenced by friends.

- Talk to your child about how difficult it is not to always go along with the crowd.
- Research has shown that children of very strict parents who have very set black and white rules are more likely to go with the crowd. Get your child to agree to matters of right and wrong by thinking for himself.
- Let your child choose his own friends and do not criticise them. You will only cause conflicts and undermine the confidence he gets from having friends who want to be with him. Do, however, make kind comments about the friends who you really like and feel are most suitable.
- Confidence can be knocked by peer pressure and bullying. These are dealt with more in Chapters 7 and 8.

Pressure from parents

Parents can quite unknowingly put pressure on their children which in turn affects their confidence. A parent putting pressure on a child to succeed can easily give the wrong message – that he is not satisfied with the achievements of the child so far. Of course, parents are really intending to be supportive and encouraging but that can so easily slip into parental pressure. Take a look at how you are encouraging your child and check that you are also reinforcing past achievements, giving plenty of praise and forming realistic expectations.

- Of course, it is important to have a positive view of your child's future but you must make sure that this does not slip into expectations which are too high. If a child feels that you are expecting more than he is capable of, the pressure will be too much and failure then becomes more likely.
- The best sort of motivation is self-motivation. Encourage your child to feel pride in his own achievements and not to be just set on pleasing you.
- Make sure you do not compare your child with others. You may ask your child how his friends have done in, say, a school test but this is really making comparisons and your child may interpret this as undue pressure.
- Together with your partner, write down what you expect from your child both now and in the future. Look at different areas such as behaviour, academic achievements and expectations for the future (such as jobs). Now make sure they are both realistic and flexible. An expectation for a child to do his best and choose a job he will enjoy is better than more specific expectations.
- If your child fails in an exam or gets low marks in a test, show sympathy and understanding. Once everyone has calmed down, talk about what went wrong and how to put it right. If you get angry or show too much disappointment, this can be interpreted as pressure too.

Coping with differences

Some children will want to blend into the background and do whatever everyone else is doing. They have no desire to be different or to stand out in a crowd. This may reflect a lack of confidence but for most children there are stages in life when it 8
is quite normal. The teenage years are a good example – teenagers seem to wear a sort of uniform and adopt a particular way of speaking. Anyone who is perceived as 'different' can find it very hard indeed.

However, some children will be different – perhaps not by choice. Your child may have a specific difficulty, be physically different or have an unusual home background. Your child will need the confidence to handle this with his peers, particularly as he gets older. In fact, it could be said that children who feel different from their peers need extra confidence.

Appearance

Your child may have something very specific such as a birthmark to cope with. Or else he may be unusually tall or short. Whatever the difference in appearance, always consider it from your child's point of view. Some children are not bothered about, say, being the tallest in the class and may even be proud of it, so do not look for problems where there are none. However, always keep an eye open for problems as they can occur at vulnerable ages.

- Let your child take the lead. If he is concerned, show that you understand but do not put ideas into his head by making an issue of any differences and implying that he should be concerned.
- Show your child that he is not different in isolation. Seek out other children with similar differences through your health visitor, doctor or even by placing an advert in the local paper.

- Join any relevant support groups if your child has a specific handicap.
- Give your child an answer to help deal with any teasing or quips. If a girl is very small, for example, she could say 'Good things come in small packages' or else another child could list one or two successful and famous short people.
- If you share a physical difference as a family – perhaps you are all very tall – then talk about the positive benefits such as being able to see at concerts.
- If there is anything practical that you can do to help such as arranging plastic surgery to help reduce a birthmark, then give it serious consideration.
- Praise your child's attributes such as his hair or eyes and ensure that he dresses in the right way to disguise his physical difference as far as possible.
- Help your child to accept his difference by talking openly about it when he needs to.

Home differences

These days there are so many types of families – from single dads to children living with grandparents – that almost anything goes and nothing is really that 'different'. However, children can still *feel* different if their particular home set-up is not the same as their friends'.

- Talk about all the different families you know, including those in the same situation as yourselves.
- Talk about the positive aspects of your particular home.
- Talk about how he can answer questions from friends, giving him specific things to say in response to teasing.
- If *you* feel different and awkward about it then your child is likely to pick up this attitude. Make sure he does not hear you making excuses for your set-up, putting yourself down or being embarrassed about it. If you are proud and confident to be who you are, then your child will find it easier to feel the same.

Other differences

Your child may have an unusual name or, if you move area, a different accent from everybody else. In fact, the possibilities of differences to cope with are endless and they can all affect confidence if you and your child allow them to. Here are some golden rules for dealing with differences.

- If your child can change the difference to be like his peers and he wants to, then let him. He may, for example, prefer to be known by his middle name. Let him – he can always go back to the unusual name you gave him later.
- Give your child something to say in response to teasing.
- Be proud and positive about the differences yourself but do acknowledge when your child finds it difficult.
- Talk about coping with it together. Do not expect your child to cope just because you did. Saying 'I got through school with the name "Ramsbottom" so you can too' does not help. Your child is not you and may need guidance.
- Similarly, if you find it difficult to cope with a difference, do not automatically assume your child will.

Parents say . . .

'People always commented about Joanna's height whenever we saw them. It was either 'You're big for your age' or 'You seem to have grown again.' Joanna became very self-conscious. In the end, I asked friends to comment about her hair instead, which she was growing. And when strangers commented on her height, we used to tell them that each generation is half an inch taller than the last. That

shut them up and made Joanna feel that it was their mistake and that she was not a freak. ’

(Mother of Joanna, 7)

‘ *I was very aware that Joe did not have a dad. Sadly, he died when Joe was only a baby. Other people assumed that we were divorced and Joe did not seem to have the confidence to put them straight. He also wanted another dad so that he was the same as his two best mates. However, I joined a branch of Cruse to meet other people in the same situation and Joe met a lot of families the same as us. He is not so self-conscious now – he knows he is not different to everyone. He has also laid off putting pressure on me to find him another dad. I would recommend anyone to join a group which will show you and your children that you are not really that different after all.* ’

(Mother of Joe, 10)

‘ *Hyacinth was fine until that programme – Keeping Up Appearances – and now all her friends call her Hyacinth Bucket! I have just heard that they are not making any more programmes but I'm quite sad. I think it has actually helped Hyacinth's confidence to have an unusual name and now she's got an answer to everything!* ’

(Mother of Hyacinth, 12, Heather, 9 and Henrietta, 7)

I remember feeling miserable when we moved when I was a child. I think that's why I expected Tom and Hannah to feel upset and I made a big thing of it. Other parents in the Parent-Link group pointed out that everything I said was negative. I kept saying 'It won't be too bad', 'Don't worry, you'll get used to it' and 'Try not to get too upset.' I was in danger of passing my anxiety on to them. Luckily, I changed tack and started talking about the good things about moving and making practical arrangements for them to look around the area. The move went very smoothly in the end.

(Mother of Tom, 8 and Hannah, 6)

I think all parents put some pressure on their children to succeed. I wish I'd been a bit more laid back as they grew up. Right from the start I wanted them to talk early, to walk early and to be the first to write their names. As teenagers, they both lack confidence and I wonder if I am to blame.

(Mother of two teenagers, aged 14 and 17)

Checklist: CAN YOUR CHILD COPE WITH CHANGES?

1 What would concern your child most if you were suddenly to move to a new area?

a He would not be concerned.
b He would miss his friends and clubs/activities.
c He would just feel generally worried about everything being different.
d Don't know.

2 Does your child cope with a sudden change in arrangements?

a Easily.
b With some concern.
c With anxiety – he likes everything to be organised in a predictable way.
d You make sure there are no sudden changes in any arrangements.

3 If your child suddenly had to wear glasses, how would he react?

a Easily. He would enjoy wearing them.
b He would be worried about what his friends would think.
c He would be self-conscious and try to avoid wearing them.
d Don't know.

4 Your child's best friend moves away. What would he do?

a Make other friends easily.
b Be very upset for a while and need help to make other friends.
c Be thrown completely and not know how to cope.
d Don't know.

5 What would cause your child the most anxiety?

a Nothing would cause all that much anxiety.
b A major change in the family or home.
c Any change at home, school or with friends.
d Don't know.

Mostly as: Everybody has some concern over changes, and you may only be looking for obvious anxiety. Always look out for it manifesting itself in different ways. Mostly bs: This shows a normal amount of concern with change but your support would help. Mostly cs: Your child needs a lot of support to cope with changes. Make sure he has some day-to-day changes to cope with so that he copes better when major changes do occur. Mostly ds: Make sure that you are not protecting your child from any changes at all. And tune into your child, observe how he copes with the little difficulties so that you know what sort of reaction to expect when any major difficulties or changes occur.

CHAPTER FIVE

Social skills

Social skills are really the outside appearance of confidence. You can be confident without having good social skills but the reaction from others will eventually knock that confidence. Equally, you can lack confidence and develop good social skills. In this case, confidence can grow from learning good social skills. There is no doubt the two are very closely linked.

So what are these social skills which can help with confidence? Basically they are the life skills we need in order to relate to other people and be accepted by them. They include manners, good communication skills, good listening skills, turn taking, sharing, and behaving in an acceptable way in a group.

Social skills have to be learnt but there is a developmental aspect too. Toddlers, for example, are naturally self-centred and the ability to consider the point of view of others comes partly with maturity. However, some people remain self-centred, talking about themselves without a thought for the listener, so clearly there is a learning process to go through too. And it's never too late – social skills can be improved at any age and parents have a very important role to play.

How social skills develop: an overview

0–1 years

Your baby will be learning that other people exist and will begin to communicate with them, albeit non-verbally. However, a baby is egocentric and will not have concern for the needs of others.

2–4 years

Toddlers are still largely egocentric and will have difficulty understanding the needs of others. So sharing and turn taking will need to be learnt. They will communicate with others but may not always listen to what others say to them. They will learn basic manners and social niceties which will be used to please you rather than for any moral reasons.

4–6 years

By the time your child starts school, she should have a sense of fairness, enabling her to share and take turns. She will have two-way conversations, listening to what the other person has to say. Friendships will be formed but there will still be arguing and fighting.

6–12 years

You should now be able to trust your child to behave appropriately in public and with others. Manners will sometimes need reminding about and she may still interrupt a conversation. However, she should be able to operate confidently in a group of her peers.

12–18 years

Adolescence can have a detrimental affect on social skills. Suddenly, your articulate eleven-year-old is grunting in response to questions from adults and is not quite behaving as you would expect an adult to in public. It will seem as if your child has to learn her social skills all over again, only now she will need one set for her friends and another for the rest of society.

Adults

Just because we reach adulthood does not mean that we have nothing to learn about social skills. Some people have great difficulty with small talk while others are aggressive rather than assertive when arguing for their rights.

Learning the basics

Learning to share

Knowing how to share will help your child to be accepted by others, which in turn helps with confidence. Sharing has to be learnt. This starts from an early age but do not expect too much before the age of three. However, right from the start you will need to explain to your child why we share. Explain 'Let John play with your train or he will be sad and have nothing to play with' or 'When you go to John's house, you play with his toys so he can play with your toys now.' Keep explanations simple and specific, avoiding general comments such as 'That's not fair.' Explain why it is not fair and keep encouraging your child to see things from a friend's point of view.

- Go for a trike ride with a friend where each child takes turns on the trike and cycles from one lamp post to the next.
- Buy brothers and sisters one big bag of crisps between them rather than a smaller one each.
- Let your child choose five toys to get out before a friend arrives, making it clear that the friend has equal access to all the chosen toys. This gives a child an opportunity to put really precious things away until sharing gets easier.

Learning to take turns

This goes hand in hand with learning to share. A typically egocentric toddler will find it hard to take turns at first and cries of 'me' and 'mine' will seem endless. Carry on explaining why your child should take turns and praise her when she does. You will need to play the part of referee first, talking the children through the activity – 'It's your turn now and when you've pushed the pram as far as the tree, it will be Jenny's turn.'

Turn taking is an important skill for communication too, after all, a conversation is really about taking turns to talk.

- Start by encouraging your children to take turns on something which they can queue up for, such as a slide.
- Try simple board games such as snakes and ladders and encourage your child to say whose go it is each time. Encourage her to be aware and interested in other players' moves and not just her own.
- Play a game which involves taking turns to speak such as Chinese Whispers. Older children could play 'I went to market . . .' where each player remembers a list of items bought and adds one more. This game encourages each child to listen to what the others are saying.

Manners and courtesy

Teach basic manners as soon as your child can say 'please' and 'thank you' or an approximate attempt. At first, your child will say them to please you and to get what she has asked for. Later, the basic courtesy words of 'sorry', 'please', 'thank you' and 'excuse me' will be almost automatic. You may get fed up with the sound of your own voice saying 'What do we say?' but stick with it – all the groundwork really does pay off later. Make sure you model good manners yourself, so your child should hear you and your partner using all the words you expect your child to use. Do praise your child when she is polite and do point out why it is good to be polite – other people will like you and so on. Courtesy is basically thinking about other people and many homes can operate with just that one basic rule – *Everyone should think about others and how it affects them.*

Your child will get a good response to being courteous and this can really help with confidence. It also gives you plenty to praise your child about, which also helps with confidence. Get together as a family and decide what is acceptable as far as courtesy is concerned. Some families may include traditional manners such as not putting your elbows on the table while others will reject this type of rule as unimportant.

The essential thing is to reach an agreement as a family so that your children know exactly what is expected. It also helps to fit in with school and the rest of society. You may have had to keep your elbows off the table as a child but times have changed. However, considering others and saying 'please', 'thank you', 'excuse me' and 'sorry' are universally considered to be essential manners. Whether you should open the door for a lady or give up your seat for an older person is a matter of family opinion. However, most people do respond very positively to traditional manners and this can boost your child's confidence in itself.

- Have a courtesy chart on the kitchen wall. Each member of the family gets a point for extra courteous behaviour – adults included!
- Play shops with younger children or role play difficult situations, such as talking to the head teacher, with older children. Emphasise the importance of basic manners and courtesy.

Learning to listen

Very young children often talk to each other without really having a conversation. One child may be talking about one thing and the other child about something else. It sounds like a conversation but listen carefully and you will hear something more like two monologues. You sometimes hear adults doing this but, happily, most children learn to listen to the other person and respond so that a true conversation takes place.

To start with you may need to remind your child to listen, asking questions to ensure that she has taken in what you have just said. Showing interest in the other speaker is all part of growing out of the egocentric phase. Children who are made to feel the centre of everything at all times tend to stay at this rather self-centred stage and consequently find conversation rather difficult later in life. An only child can be particularly vulnerable to this but it is important to encourage all children to take other people's needs into account. This includes parents, so tell your child when you are tired or want half an hour's peace to watch a favourite television programme. Being at your child's beck and call twenty-four hours a day does not necessarily make you a wonderful parent and does not teach your child that other people have needs too. So to help your child with listening as part of a conversation, help her to think of others too.

- Play 'Simon says' for careful listening. Children have to carry out the actions you say provided you said 'Simon says' first.
- Twenty questions is a good game for older children, who have to remember what everyone else has asked. Start by limiting it to something in one category such as an animal or something in the room.
- Story rounds ensure that each child has to listen to the other people playing the game. One person starts a story off and each player has to continue from where the last person left off.

Learning to like others

Good social skills enable children to make friends. It is important for a child to like other people, accepting any differences they may have. Even some adults seek friends who are replicas of themselves and can be intolerant of any major differences between them. Obviously, children will seek out friends with some of the same interests or 'something in common'. But to like others, your child must be accepting of all aspects of another's personality and circumstances.

To like others, a child must like herself too. A friendship is a two-way process and your child must believe that others will like her. To achieve this, your child must be confident that her family like her and that she has likeable traits of character. You can help by telling her that you like her and pointing out some specific things about her that you like.

- Get your child and her friends to mime their likes and dislikes for the others to guess.
- Older children can benefit from a penfriend. The penfriend cannot be judged by appearances and it helps encourage children to find out all about the other child.
- Get all the family to write down five good points about themselves and five good points about other people.

Conversation points

To be able to carry out a good, sociable conversation we need the following:

- good eye contact;
- good listening skills;
- an interest in other people;
- confidence that others will be interested in us;
- the ability to take turns and not interrupt;
- appropriate body language and tone of voice;
- the ability to ask other people questions about themselves;
- the ability to pick up signals that the other person is bored or wants to finish the conversation.

Difficult social situations

Some children may cope very well with friends they know and in familiar social situations. But different social situations require different skills. For example, more formal courtesy may be required when seeing a teacher or going for a job interview, while the ability to listen and make small talk may be needed for meeting new people at a club.

Dealing with authority confidently

Children learn from early school age to speak in two different tones – one for the playground and one for speaking to people in authority. Parents need not worry too much therefore about sloppy speech or inappropriate vocabulary – children know almost instinctively when it really is inappropriate. Even so, teenagers, in particular, may choose to use the wrong tone with authority.

The problem with speaking to authority is usually one of confidence. A child may associate it with difficult situations so it is important that she gets experience with talking to those in authority in easier situations.

- Set clear rules for who is called Mr and Miss and who can be addressed by Christian names.
- If your child gets nervous about speaking to authority figures, teach her a quick relaxation technique – take a deep breath from the diaphragm (stomach) area and let it out really slowly, dropping the shoulders and loosening the muscles as she breathes out. She can use this as she approaches the authority figure.
- Talk to your child about why courtesy is particularly important in these situations.
- Older children can be prepared for interviews with the head teacher or for a job by play acting the scene in advance.
- Talk about other social niceties such as standing up when an older person comes into the room or shaking hands when appropriate. Your child will feel more confident if she knows exactly how to behave.
- Non-verbal communication is important. Talk about standing and sitting with a good posture, head up and looking into the eyes of the person you are speaking to.

- Demonstrate bad posture and eye contact so that the message gets through. Ask your child to talk to you while you slouch and don't look at her – she will feel quite uncomfortable.
- Self-confidence helps children to feel less frightened of authority. Assertiveness helps children to stand up to authority when necessary.

Meeting new people

This can be an awkward social situation but it needn't be. Shy children find this particularly difficult and this is dealt with in Chapter 2.

- Be a good model. Let your child see you going up to new neighbours and introducing yourself.
- Praise any efforts your child makes at introducing herself to a new friend, however awkwardly she does it.
- Make sure that your child has plenty of opportunity to meet new people, whatever her age. This may involve joining new clubs – a good confidence-boosting experience.
- Younger children usually play alongside a new companion, eyeing each other up until they are ready to play together. Older children may need help with what to say to start the ball rolling.

Party games for social skills

Sometimes a game can help to get children mixing together when they do not know each other well. Or perhaps you want different age groups or adults and children to mix together. These games can break the ice and help with social skills.

Find your partner

Think of pairs of people, such as Lennon and McCartney or, for younger children favourite television characters who go together. Pin the name of one person on the back of each player who then has to find her partner by asking questions to others to find out who she is. Pictures could be used for younger children. Try to fix it so that the eventual pairs do not know each other very well and follow it with another game where partners are needed.

Group charades

Arrange the children into small groups to act out favourite television programmes without speaking.

Team games

Any team games which involve group discussion are useful. Try quizzes perhaps, or else memory games where each group has to remember items on a tray which are then taken away one at a time. Group discussion ('. . . you remember the things on the left . . .') will be needed to make the team successful.

Problem solving

Give the teams of children a problem to solve such as getting across the lounge without putting their feet on the floor. Again, this should involve quite a lot of interaction between the team members. Younger children can get into pairs to find a missing item, perhaps following clues.

Humorous games

There is nothing quite like humour to break the ice at parties. Most books on party games give examples of these. One is to put out trays of custard and jelly in an obstacle course and then send all the children out telling them they will be blindfolded and given directions to get across the room without treading in any. Of course, you take the jelly and custard away first and when the child takes off the blindfold, she will see that she was stepping over nothing. As each child finishes her go, she is encouraged to shout out the directions ('careful, step to one side now . . .') to the next child.

Question games

Games such as twenty questions where the children have to ask questions to guess what item one child has thought of are useful. Older children will enjoy murder in the dark where each player takes a card which will tell her if she is a murderer, detective or ordinary player. After roaming around in the dark the murderer will touch someone and tell her she's dead, which is the cue for that child to scream. Everyone gathers together while the detective or detectives ask questions to guess the identity of the murderer.

Role play for social skills

Role playing can help your child know what to expect and think about what to say at some specific event. The obvious example is job interviews where role playing the situation can help a child think about what sort of questions she is likely to get asked and what she might say in reply.

Of course, role play can be done as a game with children pretending to interview famous personalities or pretending to complain in a shop. Other children and adults could comment on who is the best complainer, interviewer or interviewee. Just getting your child to say, out loud, what she intends to say in a certain situation can be helpful in itself.

Join up for confidence

Children can be involved in groups from the time they attend their first parent and toddler's club. Later, your child can join a club to pursue a hobby or just take the opportunity to mix with others. Joining a social club can have great benefits for building confidence and self-esteem as it gives your child the opportunity to:

- meet and mix with new people;
- improve in a favourite sport or activity – (success helps confidence);

- take on positions of responsibility – the Guide and Scout movements are very good for this;
- practise using social skills which are put to good use in a familiar setting;
- make achievements in a non-competitive situation – again the Guide and Scout movements are good for this;
- learn skills of independence – younger children learn to be confident without mum or dad while older children may have their first trip away from home as a result of joining a club;
- feel part of a group which can give a sense of value to each child.

Parents say . . .

‘*My son always looks down when someone who he's not sure of approaches him. I've tried nagging him to look up but this seems to just make him more self-conscious. I've noticed a lot of his friends do the same and so I've approached his youth club leader to get someone in to talk to them about good communication skills. I'm sure it comes better from an expert – and someone who's not mum!*’

(Mother of Jonathan, 14)

‘*My five-year-old talks non stop – I sometimes wonder how her friends put up with it. At meal times, we are encouraging her to listen to what the rest of the family have to say. Progress is slow, but I think we're getting there.*’

(Mother of Jessie, 5)

> *I wish the Scout movement did not have such a naff image. My son does not even mention it to some of his friends and yet it's quite tough – certainly not all tying knots. He went on an outward bound course with them last year and came back more mature. I think coping away from parents for a while can do wonders for self-confidence.*
>
> *(Mother of Michael, 13)*

> *I believe that if you teach your child to look confident outwardly – to hold her head up, dress well and behave properly – then an inner feeling of confidence will follow. In other words, pretend to be confident and then suddenly you are!*
>
> *(Mother of three children aged 5, 11 and 13)*

Checklist: DOES YOUR CHILD HAVE GOOD SOCIAL SKILLS?

This checklist will give you a general idea of what to expect at each stage and whether your child has good social skills for her age. For example, you cannot expect a pre-school child to hold a long conversation with an adult friend of yours but if she says 'Hello' when your friends says 'Hello' to her then she has done very well. Do not look for perfection – if you can answer yes to most of the questions, your child has good social skills. *Remember,* your child will still be learning and developing and inconsistencies are likely.

Pre-school checklist

- Does your child say 'Please' and 'Thank you' with minimum nagging?
- Does your child look at people when she talks to them?
- Does your child respond sympathetically when another child hurts herself?
- Can your child wait while someone else has her go?
- Does your child enjoy the company of other children?
- Can your child sit at the table for the length of a family meal?
- Does your child offer you a sweet or crisp when she has some?
- Does your child know the names of at least five other children in her playgroup/nursery?
- Does your child say 'Excuse me' rather than shove someone out of the way – at least some of the time?
- Does your child say 'Hello' when you meet someone you know in the street?

Primary school age checklist

- Can you trust your child to be polite when asked to someone else's house?
- Does your child look forward to seeing all her school friends when she returns after a holiday break?
- Can your child play board games, enjoying them whether she wins or loses?
- Does your child automatically offer friends one of her sweets or crisps?
- Does your child enjoy belonging to a club?
- Does your child put up her hand to answer questions in class?
- Is your child happy to ask a teacher questions if she does not understand what is being taught?
- Does your child seem to understand when you are feeling tired or unwell?
- Would your child be happy to talk to a new child at school or a new member at a club?

- Does your child sometimes seem to enjoy the company of her friends even more than the company of her family?

Teenage checklist

- If, when out on her own, your teenager ran into one of your friends, would she say 'Hello' or even have a short conversation?
- Does your teenager enjoy team games?
- Does your teenager belong to a group or club with other teenagers?
- Is your teenager happy to answer the phone and make phone calls to friends?
- Does your teenager know how to introduce two people?
- Would your teenager help to make a new school chum or member of the club feel welcome?
- Is your child able to talk about more than the one or two subjects of particular interest to her?
- Would your teenager be able to stop herself from joining in with the anti-social behaviour of the rest of the group?
- Can your teenager stand up for herself in an argument without getting aggressive?
- Are you confident that your teenager uses good manners when required even if they seem to have been dropped at home?

CHAPTER SIX

The early years

Confidence grows out of positive life experiences. But it can also be knocked down at any time, again by life's experiences. Personality does have a part to play of course and some children are more susceptible to a lack of confidence than others. However, as a general rule babies are born with the capacity to be confident. If that is nurtured in the early years, then a child will cope with life's ups and downs without his self-esteem being affected. The pre-school years are therefore crucial for building a child's confidence. There is no need to wait until things go wrong before you act. Instead of concentrating on building up your child's confidence when it gets knocked down, focus on maintaining good confidence all the time. Starting early gives your child the head start he needs so do not wait for problems, have a policy for building confidence right from the start.

A confidence-building policy

If you decide right from the start that you are going to help your child be confident, then you might want to write down your 'policy' and talk to your partner and others who care for your child so that you all have the same aims. The following points should form the basis of your approach.

- Make your child feel liked and loved by those who know him.
- Make your child feel good about his achievements.
- Make your child feel good about his appearance.
- Make your child feel secure about what behaviour is expected from him.
- Make sure your child can develop at his own pace with encouragement rather than 'pushiness'.
- Make sure that your child feels secure in approaching new situations.
- Make your child's life as happy as possible but not by over-protecting him from problems.
- Make sure that your child has opportunities for developing confidence in social situations.
- Discipline for safety, security and socially acceptable behaviour without using put-downs or confidence-knockers.
- Focus on changing your child's behaviour, not his personality.

How not to be a competitive parent

Watching your child develop from a baby into a young person is one of the most enjoyable and fascinating parts of parenting. It can also cause some worries as you wait to see if your child walks, talks and does everything else at an appropriate time. It is easy to let this anxiety spill over into competition. Of course you will be proud if he reaches milestones early and of course you will worry if he seems to be doing everything later than his friends. But if you let yourself get too competitive, you could end up pushing your child on before he is ready. This can leave even a very young child with a sense of failure. You may also feel that your child has failed and he can pick up these feelings as well as the feeling that there is pressure on him to perform.

- Familiarise yourself with child development and the fact that there is a wide timescale of when children should reach their milestones. Being slow to walk, for example, does not mean that he is backward in any way.

- If you feel development is slow, discuss it with your health visitor before your child is affected by your anxiety.
- Make a list of your child's strengths and weaknesses. It is easy to see if he is slow to talk or walk but perhaps he is good at manipulating objects, building bricks or is very affectionate.
- Think of all the school children you know. Guess which ones reached their milestones early – you can't. And if you try you'll probably be wrong.
- Remember all the things which affect development – family history (if you were late with, say, crawling or with your first teeth then your child is more likely to be), gender (girls are earlier at most things than boys), position in the family (first children are usually earlier) and just the fact that all children are different.
- Do not compare your child with his friends.
- Never blame yourself if your child seems slower in one area. Confident parents make confident children.
- Write down all that you want for your child and then go back over your list, crossing out anything which is competitive, from wanting him to be the brightest at nursery to having a career mapped out for him.
- Enjoy watching your child develop at his own pace.

Help – I'm a new parent

Confidence grows from confidence, so if you have no confidence as a parent, then it will be harder to raise confident children. As a new parent you may feel lost but you know more than you think – there's a lot to be said for instinctive parenting. Most of what you do to care for your child will come automatically so if it works, then give yourself a pat on the back rather than worry whether you are doing it right. You can also consult the experts but you will hear (and read) some differing opinions, so at the end of the day you have to use your own common sense to decide what is and is not good advice.

- Try not to see problems where there are none. For example, if your baby is happy, content and putting on the right amount of weight then you are doing a good job with feeding and need not worry.
- Know what to expect. It helps to know what the normal stages of development are and what problems are so common as to be considered normal. All babies cry when they are hungry, all toddlers have tantrums and no parent gets through the potty training stage without the odd wet pair of pants.
- Decide with your partner how to deal with behaviour and then both adopt the same approach.
- Do not expect too much from your child or from yourself. There is no such thing as the perfect child and no such thing as the perfect parent. You will inevitably make mistakes, but they can be put right.
- Talk about parenting with your partner and consult your health visitor or appropriate expert if you have any problems. This is not a sign of failure.
- Concentrate on what is good about your child and focus on the good times. Remind yourself what a good job you are doing.
- Allow your child to benefit from your confidence. If you waver over discipline or seem unsure about how to cope with his tears and tantrums, he will sense that uncertainty.

Baby confidence

Babies cannot usually be thought of as lacking in confidence. However, bad experiences could effect self-esteem later. Confidence comes from a feeling of security and self-worth, both of which can be established in the early years. Your baby will cry when he needs something and as a parent you will automatically try to respond to that need. Discipline does not really come into play yet, as babies cannot be naughty on purpose. The main problem your baby will have to cope with during the first year is separation from you. Before about seven months, this has little effect. He may protest when you leave the room but is easily distracted and can be left with another carer. However, from the age of seven months fear of separation, followed by a fear of strangers, begins. This can last into the second year and leaving your baby with a babysitter or unfamiliar carer can be difficult.

There will be times during the first eighteen months when you will need to be firm – mainly with yourselves. All babies go through a fear of strangers but this does not mean that you cannot go out with your partner for the evening. It just means that you have to be aware of likely problems so that you can handle them appropriately. The same goes for other problems such as night waking. You can be firm in settling your baby into a workable routine but reassuring at the same time. Confidence may come from security but it does not come from running around after your baby for twenty-four hours a day with no thought for your own needs.

- A routine helps your baby to feel secure and to know what to expect. It also helps you to feel confident as a parent.
- Be aware of the separation/fear of strangers stage. Spend some time together with a babysitter before you go out so that if your baby wakes at night he sees a familiar face.
- Find out what works for your child. It may help to spend time settling him in with the child minder or it may help to make goodbyes as brief as possible.
- Reassure your baby whenever he is upset or distressed about anything. If you are trying to change a habit such as night waking, this reassurance may be brief but it will still be reassuring for your child to know that you are around.
- Allow your child to have a special toy, blanket or even his

thumb as a comforter, especially when you are not there. Purchase a duplicate in case of emergencies.

- Do not be a clingy parent. Encourage other involved adults to build up close relationships with your baby.
- Have a more rigid, predictable routine for difficult times of the day such as going to bed.
- Remember that you cannot really spoil a young baby.

Toddler confidence

The main confidence knocker in toddlerhood is inappropriate discipline. Your toddler will be learning which behaviour is acceptable and which is not. He will then test the rules and test you just to make sure. At the same time, he will be developing his first skills of independence, but frustration is inevitable as his ideas will be bigger than his ability. And just to make matters even more complicated, limited communication skills will add to the frustration.

Inevitably then, discipline will pay a key part in bringing up a toddler. Confidence can be knocked, however, if it is all discipline and no praise. At this stage parenthood can seem an endless battle with tantrums and poor behaviour. And for your child, it can seem as if he can do nothing right. It is essential therefore to praise your child at every opportunity and to tell him how much you like him. This confidence-building strategy can then set the necessary discipline in balance.

Praise your toddler

This can sound obvious but it is all too easy to fall into the trap of ignoring your toddler's good behaviour while giving your full attention to his bad behaviour. Not only can this affect his self-esteem and feeling of self-worth but it makes bad behaviour more likely. Bad behaviour can become the best way of getting your attention. A typical scene might be a toddler sitting quietly colouring in a picture. Mum, pleased to see her toddler occupying himself, takes the opportunity to sort out the kitchen cupboard. Eventually the toddler gets fed up and applies his crayons to the wall, knowing that the last time he did that mum came running. And that's just what mum does.

However, add a little praise to the situation and a toddler can feel good about himself and bad behaviour can be avoided. If your child is playing nicely tell him how pleased you are and offer some reward if he carries on while you clear the cupboard out. Keep going to your toddler, not to check on him but to tell him how nice his picture is. And when he gets bored, involve him in your task. One happy toddler, one happy mother.

Rules for praising your toddler

- Praise for effort as well as achievement.
- Do not restrict praise for one thing, such as drawing or being able to count to ten. Praise him for playing nicely, for getting his own socks on, for carrying his cup well and so on.
- Do not create 'party tricks' by over-praising something rather cute such as mispronouncing a word. This might not sound so cute a year ahead.
- Do not just praise what your child does. Praise him for the sort of person he is – perhaps he is caring towards other children or animals or perhaps he has a great sense of humour. And don't forget to tell him that you like being with him.
- Use praise as a cushion for criticism. So rather than say 'Can't you be quiet for one minute?', you might try 'I love hearing you talk but you have to learn to listen too.'
- Praise your child whenever he is being good. This makes it easier for both of you when you need to reprimand – you won't feel like you're always nagging and hopefully he won't feel like he's always being nagged.

Discipline and self-esteem

You will need to discipline your toddler as he is now learning what is right and wrong. Toddlers feel more secure with well-defined boundaries and security helps confidence. However, you will need to put some thought into how you are going to discipline your toddler so that you are consistent both with yourself and with others dealing with him.

Rules for disciplining your toddler

- Show your disapproval of the *action* and not your toddler as a person. 'You did something very silly' is better than 'You are very silly.'
- Always give short, clear explanations at the time of the wrong-doing. 'Don't hit John; it hurts and makes him cry' is better than just 'Don't be a bully.' 'Because I say so' is *not* a reason.
- Do not assume that your toddler should have known better. He is still learning what the boundaries are. Start by giving a firm 'No' together with an explanation.
- The next time, you may want to give a warning such as 'If you do that again, then we will go home' but you must carry out any threats that you make.
- Where possible ignore bad behaviour, especially if it is to get your attention. Once he starts behaving appropriately, give him your full attention.
- Decide on what punishment you will use. For toddlers it has to be immediate. Saying 'You won't go to the park on Sunday' is not very useful as he will have forgotten the incident by the weekend.
- Smacking is immediate but rarely works in the long term. It just teaches your child that problems can be solved by hitting. Research shows that many toddlers get confused about why they have been smacked.
- Never threaten a loss of love or make love conditional. Saying

'I don't like silly boys' or 'I'll really love you if you stop doing that' will badly affect self-esteem.
- Time out is useful. You can remove your toddler to a quiet corner away from the action for ten minutes while strongly showing your disapproval.
- Consistent bad behaviour can sometimes be dealt with by rewarding the good. For example, you could have a star chart with a star earned for each day your toddler does not bite (or even half day if this is too challenging). A reward can be given at the end of three or four days.
- Make sure that your toddler knows that your love is unconditional and that however naughty he has been, you still love him even if you haven't liked some of the things he has done.

Toddler tantrums

Toddler tantrums are a major reason why your child may end up getting more negative reinforcement than positive. Tantrums are a part of being a toddler and they do pass – eventually. Handling them sensitively will make the difference between your toddler knowing that he is loved despite these bouts of temper and feeling that he is nothing but a nuisance.

- Do not blame yourself for tantrums – all toddlers have them.
- Avoid tantrums whenever possible. If, for example, you see that your toddler is going to have a tantrum about putting on his coat, just tuck it under your arm and take it with you until your toddler seems more calm.
- Take every opportunity when there is no tantrum going on to tell your toddler that you love him and like being with him.
- Show your toddler that you understand how he feels. There are story books about tantrums which may help.
- Tantrums can be quite frightening for a child who has, after all, lost control of himself. Ignore them while they are going on but be ready for an understanding cuddle straight afterwards.

- Whatever happens, remain calm yourself. When you start to get tense, let your partner step in while you unwind in a hot bath. Tantrums are easier to deal with if you feel relaxed and in control.

Sibling rivalry and confidence

So often it is during the toddler years that another baby comes along and it is easy for a toddler to feel pushed out. If a toddler gets the wrong message – that you seem to prefer looking after this new baby – then confidence can really take a knocking. Even if your toddler is the youngest, it is at this time that he has to learn to share and one of the most difficult things to share is mum.

New baby drill

- Prepare your toddler for a new baby using story books to help. Make sure, as far as possible, he knows what to expect.
- Get your toddler involved with the new baby – never over-protect your baby from an eager toddler with cries of 'Don't touch!' Keep calm and help your toddler to learn how to handle the baby.
- Give your toddler special jobs such as putting the powder on or fetching the nappy.
- Try to have time on your own with your toddler and tell him how much you value that time.
- Do not be annoyed about sibling rivalry. Of course you need to make it clear that you do not tolerate aggression towards a baby brother or sister, but you can show that you understand too.
- Make sure other people do not fall into the trap of showering attention on to a new baby and ignoring the toddler.
- Tell everyone how helpful your toddler is with the new baby – and make sure he hears.

Squabble squashers

As brothers and sisters grow up together, arguments and a certain amount of rivalry are inevitable. Hopefully, they will be the best of friends some of the time, but remember that one sibling can knock the confidence of a younger or weaker sibling if rivalry gets out of hand.

- Spend some time with each child on their own whenever possible.
- One child may be experiencing some difficulty which takes up a lot of your time and attention. Make sure you compensate by spending more time with the other children too.
- Do not compare one child with another.
- Do not encourage situations where direct rivalry is inevitable. If possible, encourage them to pursue different hobbies and if, say, they both want to learn a musical instrument, then try to get them to choose different ones.
- At some time one of your children is bound to accuse you of loving the other one more. Dismiss this immediately but note that this child seems insecure and do some standard confidence boosting. Especially tell him how much he is loved.
- Encourage all your children to have friends around. You cannot expect them to enjoy each other's company twenty-four hours a day.
- Do not worry, squabbling does pass.

What not to say to your toddler

'Oh, you're so cack-handed, let me do it!' Instead you could say, 'You're doing really well. Now, if I give you just a little hand, you'll be there. Well done.'
'Can't you see I'm busy? Now find something to do!' Instead try, 'Come and help me while I sort this washing out, then we'll see what you want to do.'
'You are so careless. Look at this mess!' Try instead, 'Thank you

for trying to help. Next time remember to carry it with both hands.'
'Don't do that or I'll be very cross!' It might be better to say 'Don't do that or you might fall and hurt yourself.'
'Oh all right, have some sweets if it will stop you moaning.' Instead try 'When you have stopped moaning, I will think about it' and then ignore the whining.
'I love you, so surely you can be good.' Love is unconditional and should not be used for threats or bribery.
'Don't be a baby' or *'Grow up.'* Toddlers are not grown up and will still regress to baby-like habits every now and then. Try to find out if there is something wrong. Or perhaps you have been expecting too much from your toddler recently.
'Play properly!' There is no such thing as playing 'properly'. If your toddler is happy and busy then what is the problem. Toddlers learn through all sorts of play and you will knock his confidence if he is made to feel that he can only play in a certain way.
'Get off, I'm all ready to go out!' Better to say 'I love having a cuddle with you but my new dress might get creased. Let me give you a big kiss instead.' Never reject physical contact from your toddler.
'You're so untidy.' It is better to avoid labelling your child so say 'Your room is so untidy' instead.
'What do you look like?' If your child has made an effort to dress himself then he need hear nothing but praise.
'He can be so embarrassing. I can't take him anywhere.' Do not say anything about your toddler to friends which you would not say to his face. He does have ears and understands more than he can say himself.

What not to do to your toddler

- Don't do things for your toddler, such as his fastenings, when he is learning to do them himself. Give just the right amount of help necessary and praise any effort he makes.
- Don't stop praising him as soon as he can do something. Keep encouraging him to use the skills of independence he has learnt.

- Don't expect too much. Some days your toddler will seem to want you to do everything for him and on other days he will want to do it all himself. Accept the up-and-down nature of the toddler years.
- Don't take it for granted that your toddler just knows you love him. Everyone needs and likes to be told every now and then.
- Don't reprimand your toddler for being shy occasionally. Just be there when he needs you and back off when he is ready to cope alone.
- Don't pile the praise on your toddler and nobody else. Making him the centre of attention when it comes to achievements indirectly puts pressure on him. Let him hear you praise others too.
- Don't keep your toddler to yourself. Encourage him to mix with other toddlers, perhaps at a toddler group, even though they may not truly play together yet. Get him used to being with other adults too. This will help with his confidence later on and prepares him for nursery or playgroup.
- Don't get annoyed when your toddler is frightened of something, however unreasonable his fear seems to be. He needs reassurance and understanding. Toddler fears are very common.
- Don't wait for your toddler to cuddle you. Even if he is going through a very independent stage, physical contact is very important.
- Don't laugh at him at the wrong moment. This can be difficult to judge but generally it is best not to laugh when his efforts go wrong or when he makes mistakes. Unless you know he will laugh along with you, of course.
- Don't expect to get it right every time. This is a difficult stage for parents as well as for children, and you are bound to feel irritated at times. Your toddler will not be harmed by the occasional 'mistake'.

Parents say . . .

'I think toddlers can be confident overall but have moments of low confidence. I think we forget that so much is new to them. I took Camilla swimming in a pool we've never been to before with flumes and rapids and even a giant plastic crocodile. It's not surprising she wouldn't let go of me. Perhaps it would be stranger if she just accepted all these new things with no reaction at all!'

(Mother of Camilla, 3)

'Perhaps we need to give our toddlers permission to have tantrums. If we say 'It's OK have a good scream and get it out of your system' we don't get so het up and they get over it quickly and then life can carry on.'

(Father of Jonathan, 2½)

'John was so jealous of the new baby that I really felt angry with him. Of course, that just made it worse. The health visitor told me not to drop everything when the baby cried and rush off to him, especially if I was playing with John. Instead I calmly say 'Oh no, the baby's crying, let's go and see what's wrong and then we can finish our story in peace.' John helps me and so does not feel suddenly abandoned.'

(Mother of John, 3 and Simon, 6 months)

> *I pushed my older child on as quickly as possible and I think it left him feeling as if he had to do well to please me. I was more laid back with my younger children as toddlers and now they are not always looking for my approval. They have enough confidence to do it for themselves and feel pride in their own achievements.*
>
> *(Mother of three children – 5, 11 and 13)*

> *I feel really proud that Jessie will talk to anyone and is so outgoing. I feel sure it's because she went to a child minder from an early age and so has got used to being with lots of different people.*
>
> *(Mother of Jessie, 5)*

Checklist: DOES YOUR CHILD GET THE RIGHT MESSAGE?

What messages are you really giving your toddler when you say the following? (The confidence-crushing messages are given in italics.)

1. 'Slow down and speak properly.' *(I don't like the way you talk. I wish you talked differently – or perhaps not at all.)*
2. 'But you're my big girl now.' *(You have been replaced by another baby and you lose all the privileges being a baby brings.)*
3. 'But that's supposed to be a cooker not a car.' *(I don't like the way you are playing.)*

4 'You're not going to the park because you pushed your sister last week.' (*You are not going to the park* – the bad deed was too long ago for a toddler to make a connection. He may even think you are not taking him to the park because you don't like him.)

5 'Stop screaming or I'll have to take you out of the trolley and carry you.' (*If you scream, you'll get my full attention, which is what you want.*)

6 'We don't allow that sort of behaviour here and the consequence will be that you will not be allowed to play with Kevin and Julian again. After all, they are very upset and it is really your fault because of what you did.' (No message will be received from this. Keep explanations short and simple.)

7 'You're just like your brother.' (*I expect you to be like your brother and do not expect you to change.*)

8 'Stop annoying me.' (*I am annoyed with you* – however, your child will not know why or how to put it right.)

9 'I don't like little girls who fidget.' (*I don't like you.*)

10 'Why can't you be like your brother?' (*I prefer your brother.*)

CHAPTER SEVEN

Confidence at school – success and failure

Hopefully your child will start school with enough confidence to see her through the inevitable ups and downs of education. And ups and downs there most definitely will be. At school, children have to learn to cope with making and losing friends, success and failure in all aspects of school life and facing new people and situations. There are bound to be times when confidence wavers so be prepared to step in with confidence boosters when they are needed.

Parental awareness is very important so that you know very quickly when your child's confidence needs boosting. Suddenly you may feel that you have lost control as your child will be out of your sight for most of the day. Your child will be coming home tired and not always in the mood to regurgitate the day's events. This will leave you feeling left in the dark. Inevitably, you may see problems where there are none or blow minor problems out of all proportion. It is easy to panic when your child comes home upset, particularly when you have been used to witnessing any upsets first hand and therefore in a more able position to deal with them readily. Suddenly you do not understand the circumstances or know the people involved. How can you possibly help? First, be understanding and secondly be sure to keep the lines of communication open between you and your child. And at all times, you need to be aware of your child's feelings and read the non-verbal clues she gives out when she comes home or talks about school.

Parent awareness

- Make yourself familiar with your child's school environment. If you have seen the classroom, it is easier to visualise her there when she describes the events of the day.
- Familiarise yourself with your child's teacher and as many school friends as you can.
- Recognise symptoms of tiredness. You may easily confuse fatigue with being upset. And remember that any problems your child does have will be compounded by tiredness. So let your child have an energy-boosting snack and then relax before calmly talking about problems together.
- Watch for non-verbal clues that show your child needs to talk to you. Is she 'hovering' about? Or does she keep asking you obvious questions indicating that there is something more she wants to say to you?
- If your child has been upset at school or had her confidence knocked, it can manifest itself in many different ways. Learn to recognise the symptoms in your own child. Perhaps she becomes aggressive or else withdrawn. Not all children come home, burst into tears and then tell you all about it.
- Let your child talk when she is ready. Sometimes she may prefer to wait until a quiet time at the end of the day. However, try not to let your child go to sleep with a worry. It is better to be able to reassure your child before bedtime.

Parent attitude

You will want your child to have a positive attitude to school as this can certainly help with confidence. It is essential, therefore, to have a positive attitude towards school yourself. Try to forget about your own past experiences. Parents can be influenced by the fact that they hated school. Schools have changed and you can expect your child to enjoy at least some of it. Do not air your own negative feelings about school or your child will not expect anything enjoyable to come out of it at all.

Be realistic. While you can expect your child to have a positive attitude to school in general, you cannot expect her to love everything about it. She may not enjoy sport or cooking. Accept her dislikes and point out all the things she does enjoy and what she is gaining from school. Do your best to curb your own nerves. When your child first starts school, moves up a class or goes on to secondary school, you may feel nervous or even anxious. However, your child will sense your anxiety so try to give out positive vibrations and talk about any changes in an optimistic and positive way. Although your positive attitude will help your child, do acknowledge her own negative thoughts or anxiety. You will want both to reassure your child and show her that you understand.

Do not be a clingy parent. This can happen when your child first starts school – of course you will miss her but she will sense if you do not really want her to go. You may even enjoy your child's clinginess as it shows you that she loves you. You must stop the need to cling on to this part of your child's life. Write down all the positive things about your child being at school and separating from you – include the benefits to you as well as your child.

Help your child to have a positive attitude to school

In the first instance, try to make sure that you have a positive attitude yourself (see above). Where possible, give positive responses to moans and worries, so if your child says 'I hate maths', point out the things she does like, the things she is good at, and find out if she is having any specific problems you can help with. Just saying 'Well, everyone has to do maths' is not helpful, understanding or reassuring.

Give your child positive feedback on her achievements but make sure you do not just focus on academic achievements. Tell her how good her painting is and hang it on the wall. Tell her she looks lovely in her uniform. And most of all, tell her how much you like her. Find something which your child is successful at – easy for the academic or sporty child. If your child seems to be under-achieving, enlist the teacher's help in finding something she can feel successful with.

Recognise the social aspect of school life. You may see school as a means to an end – good exam results and a job – but for your child it will be the centre of her social life. Encourage your child to have friends home and make a point of getting to know them. A child with friends at school will have a more positive attitude to school in general.

What not to say . . .

'All teachers are the same – you just have to put up with them.'
'You just don't try . . .'
'Your friends seem able to manage – why can't you?'
'When I was at school . . .'
'You'll never get a job at this rate.'
'You're going to grow up to be just like . . .'
'All girls are the same.'
'You're just not the academic type, I suppose.'
'Whatever you do goes wrong!'
'You probably won't pass but do your best anyway.'
'That's just typical . . .'

What to say to your child's negative comments

'I can't do this!' You can empathise and then offer practical advice in a positive tone. So you might say 'That certainly looks hard, but I'm sure if we take it step by step and I talk you through the first step then you can manage. Once you've done one, the rest will seem easier.'

'I'm not asking the teacher. She'll just get cross and blame me.' Again, you can empathise, offer positive, practical advice and help your child to see the teacher's point of view. So you might say 'Yes, it must be very frustrating if you don't get a good response from your teacher. Teachers are always rushed and busy. Perhaps if you picked a better time and I helped you think out exactly what to say.'

'What do you know about it. You wouldn't understand.' With empathy and positive advice you can even help with this common negative comment. You might try saying 'Only you know how you feel but if you tell me more about it, I can try to understand. Two heads are better than one and I might be able to help.'

'I hate school.' You might say 'School can be tough at times but if we work out all the things you like and dislike about school, perhaps we can think about how to make the things you dislike a bit better.'

'No one likes me.' You might say 'It can feel like that sometimes and there's nothing worse than thinking that you haven't a friend. But let's think of some of the people you have got on with in the past. The children who have invited you to their parties must like you. Perhaps it would help to invite some children home so you can get to know each other better.' You will want to add your own view – 'I like you and I really enjoyed your company at the park earlier. I am sure that other children must see this nice side of you too.'

Confidence from independence

Children can gain confidence at school by being able to do things for themselves. The child who has to have help with her coat or who is used to relying on a parent to get everything organised can soon lose confidence at school. It is important to prepare your child for school so that she already has the necessary skills and is used to coping without a parent present (see Chapter 6).

When your child starts school, it is easy to mother her more than usual as a way of compensating for her leaving your side all day. You might be tempted to dress her in the morning or get everything ready for her. You will be doing her no favours. If she is used to being independent at home, she will find it easier to be independent at school.

How to help

- Make it easy – choose shoes with easy fastenings, zip-up coats and a lunch box that opens easily.
- Give your child plenty of time. If you are rushed you will end up doing things for her.
- Expect your child to do things for herself and she will expect to do them too.
- Give just enough help and no more. No need to let your child get frustrated with her shoe fastenings – start her off and let her do the rest.
- Give plenty of praise. Do not take it for granted that your child will do things for herself – praise her when she does or if she has a go.

Decisions, decisions

Your child will feel a sense of independence if she is allowed to make some of her own decisions. This helps with confidence as you can show her that her views have value. Listen to your child's opinions when you make family decisions such as where to go on holiday or what to have for lunch. Always take them seriously even if you do not use her idea. So you might say 'That's a good idea – Australia sounds wonderful. I don't think we can afford it this year but hopefully we can go in the future.' Don't put her ideas down or dismiss them straight away. So don't say 'Don't be ridiculous, you know we can't possibly go to Australia!' Laughing at her ideas has the same effect.

Some decisions can be left to your child completely but you

must let go. It is no good deciding that your child can wear whatever she wants at weekends, for example, if you then criticise her choice (a good confidence knocker) or change the rules just because Auntie Janet is coming to stay.

Let your child decide . . .

Who her friends are.
What to wear at home.
What hobbies she wants to pursue.
How she has her hair.
How she spends her leisure time.
How she arranges her own space – normally her bedroom.

Let her have a say when . . .

You buy her new clothes.
You decide on an outing or holiday.
You decorate or re-arrange her bedroom.
And where she does her homework.
To invite someone home (and who).
You make any major family decision.

Solving problems

Helping your child to become independent will also include helping her to solve her own problems. You are not always going to be there when she has problems and she must gradually learn to deal with them herself. However, it is a gradual process and she will still need your support and understanding. During the school years, the emphasis will be on discussing problems together and helping your child to decide what to do, rather than sorting it all out for her.

How to help

- Have a more positive view of problems. You may want to protect your child from problems when in fact she will gain a lot from having to solve and deal with them.
- Do not pretend to your child, or to yourself, that life is always easy. Let her know that life has problems and that you too have fears and worries sometimes.
- Set a good example. Do not let your child see you in a panic over worries and concerns.
- Get involved with your child's problem in an appropriate way for the age and personality of your child. Younger children will need more direct action. Older children will still need sympathy and sometimes practical advice.

Action plan for helping with a problem

1. Be sympathetic and understanding. This may involve telling your child that you had similar problems at her age.
2. Keep the lines of communication open. Make sure you are available to listen to your child's problems when she needs to talk.
3. Decide if your child can be left to solve the problem herself or if she will need more direct action from you.
4. Help your child to solve the problem herself by getting her to organise her thoughts. Perhaps she has a difficult choice to make in which case she could write down the pros and cons of each option.
5. Get your child to think about it. This may involve a younger child drawing pictures and an older child writing her thoughts down. It will certainly involve your child talking about her emotions.
6. Help your child to come up with some concrete actions which she could take to help with the problem.
7. Help your child to see her problem in relation to the rest of her life and to keep it in proportion.

For example . . .
Perhaps your child has fallen out with a friend at school.

1 Show that you understand. Do not say 'Well, you are a bit bossy' or 'I expect it was something you said.' You can tell her about how you fell out with a friend, either when you were young or more recently with a friend at work. This will show her that it happens to everyone and that it can be put right.
2 Have a quiet time at the end of each day for a 'chat'. Look for non-verbal clues that your child wants to talk about it. Perhaps she is hovering around or waiting to be asked why she is looking so miserable.
3 If your child has had arguments like this before then leave her to it. If this is a new experience or if it seems to be dragging on longer than usual, you may need to sit down and tackle it together.
4 Get your child to talk about the options – she could wait for the other girl to apologise, she could apologise herself, she could invite her friend home etc. Think about the pros and cons of each option.
5 Get her to write down exactly what happened. This may help her to take some of the blame or responsibility.
6 Get your child to talk about the problem of just moping about and the advantages of taking action.
7 A problem may lead to negative thoughts, so in this case your child may say something like 'No one likes me.' It is important to help your child to keep this one argument in proportion and reassure her that a lot of other people, including yourself, like her and enjoy her company.

Of course, some problems are going to be more 'serious' than this – children may have to deal with divorce and death as well as the day-to-day problems of life. However, never dismiss your child's problem as trivial. If it worries your child then take it seriously. Constant reminders of how lucky your child is or about the starving and homeless people of the world rarely help when there is a crisis. However, if you can get your child to list all the good things about herself and her life, then she may begin to get things in proportion. And having to deal with problems helps in itself. After all, once your child has experienced the ease with which you can make up with a friend, it won't seem quite so devastating the next time.

Confidence-building activities

At school, your child will have the opportunity to get involved with different activities and clubs. Some of these are very good for building confidence. If your child can find an activity which she is good at so much the better – there is nothing better than success for boosting confidence. However, some children respond better to non-competitive activities, gaining confidence from the experience rather than the success. It may be that just the social experience of participating in an activity helps with confidence. Maybe it will be the experience of standing up and performing in front of others which will help. Whatever the reason, do note when something specific is helping and encourage her as much as you can. Of course, some activities can have an adverse effect. When it comes to extra curricular activities, you must remind yourself that they are primarily for your child's pleasure and that the choice of activity is hers.

Beware of . . .

- Pushing your child into an activity which you enjoy or which you wish you had done as a child.
- Pushing your child into an activity because you think it is good for her when she is clearly not interested. It may be good for her to perform in front of others but if acting is not for her, there are alternatives.
- Forcing your child to stick with an activity which she does not like. However, make sure that your child is not giving up for

some other reason such as falling out with a friend. This can be put right.

- Pushing your child into being competitive. Some children are happy to participate on a non-competitive level and can gain confidence this way. However, beware of a fear of failure – this may indicate that her general confidence needs boosting.
- Putting too much emphasis on the success rather than the general enjoyment of the activity.

Which activities?

Drama

This can be done at any age and is largely non-competitive. Some children feel more confident when they are being someone else and this feeling of confidence can then spread out into the rest of their lives. Drama will include skills of speaking and communication which are important for confidence and your child can also experience being part of a social group.

Drama will be part of the school curriculum, so if your child shows a particular interest in this subject, then you can suggest that she joins a local group. Ask your local librarian about classes for children. Find out more about each group as some will be just for fun while others may involve taking tests in speech and drama. Some clubs may put an emphasis on group activities while others will encourage your child to perform to the rest of the group and to parents.

Sport

If your child has a particular interest in a sport, then she may want to join a club out of school. This may be linked to her school but even if it is not, there are bound to be other children from her school whom she knows. Sport can help your child with social skills as well as lead to opportunities for team leadership – a great confidence booster.

Debating

This is most suitable for older children and, like drama, can give your child the opportunity to speak out in public. Some children find that they can gain confidence by speaking out in this prepared way which then helps when they are speaking in less formal situations. Your child is most likely to become involved in debating through school, though in some areas local clubs do exist.

Elocution

It is unlikely that this will be your child's choice of activity. Are you sure you are not wanting to push your child into it as a way of gaining confidence? It can certainly help, but it is important that your child feels positive about taking elocution lessons. If not, a drama class with an emphasis on speaking skills may be a good compromise.

Music and dance

These activities can also involve performing in public, which can help with confidence. If your child can take a part, however small, in a performance of any kind then she will feel a boost of adrenalin and a feeling of success. Your child will learn to cope with nerves and fear and when everything goes well will get nothing but praise.

School problems and how to help

Bullying

Bullying is very strongly linked to confidence – or lack of it. If your child is being bullied, her confidence is bound to be affected and if the bullying is allowed to continue for long periods, then it can take a lot of time and effort to help your child get her confidence back again. The bullier, too, has a problem with confidence. It may be that it is your child doing the bullying and this is a sign that she has a problem. Children who bully often lack confidence themselves and have difficulty making friends. They deal with their own problems by trying to exert control over another child. Sometimes the bullier has been bullied herself and is making sense of this by turning the tables on someone else. Bullying can start in the pre-school years, although parents and nursery teachers are not always prepared to call it bullying.

Bullying can take several forms. A child can be physically or mentally bullied – making continuous offensive remarks about someone's appearance is certainly bullying. Bullying can be carried out by groups of children or by individuals and tends to be more than a one-off incident. The bullying often happens every day and leaves the victim feeling unhappy, helpless and sometimes very frightened.

Possible signs

- Your child tells you directly. Always take it seriously and never say 'Just ignore them' or 'It'll pass.' If bullying is nipped in the bud, it can save your child's confidence from being completely shattered.
- Your child tells you indirectly. Perhaps she tells you that she does not like walking to school with her friends any more or that she wants to stop attending an after-school club.
- Appearance. Your child has ripped clothes or books or even bruises and scratches.
- Mood. Your child is suddenly unhappy and feels ill in the mornings. Perhaps she does not want to go to school.
- Unexplained events. Your child loses some of her possessions.

What to do

Go straight to the school. Most schools have a sensitive policy for dealing with bullying. Show your child that you understand and tell her that something must be done to put it right. Explain to your child that it is the bullier who has problems, not her, and that the bullier likes her reactions and that it is better not to react at all.

Give your child some strategies for dealing with bullying. This will include ignoring the bullier, using positive body language to show that she does not mind, having a quip ready as a reply – humour can help, as can sticking together with a friend. If you know the other child's family, then you may want to talk it through with them. Do not go around accusing the other child but talk it through as a whole problem which you can all discuss and tackle together. Get in touch with Kidscape who can give you more information about bullying and how to help (address at the back of the book).

When bullying has knocked confidence

Make an effort to invite other children round to show your child that she is liked. If your child has been bullied about a particular physical attribute, then help her to get this in proportion. If she has been called 'fatty', then show her that it was not her weight that led her to be bullied but the reaction the bulliers got from her. There are probably larger girls who have not been bullied.

Tell your child that you like her and that no one really likes people who bully. Keep up discussions with the school even after the bullying has stopped and praise her when she starts to tackle the bullying problem well.

If your child is bullying

Do not accuse your child until you know the facts and then try to tackle the problem in an understanding way. Saying 'You must be very unhappy to have behaved like this' may open up the discussion. Children who bully tend to have a low self-esteem. You need to build up your child's confidence and to show her that she can make friends. You could try inviting the child who she has bullied round to play. This can help both children overcome the difficulty. Your child will need to apologise and understand what she has done and how it has affected the other person.

Bullying can also be done by spoilt children who are used to getting their own way at home – often by bullying their parents! Ensure that your child is able to take the needs of other members of the family into account.

Truancy

The school should let you know if your child has been playing truant and you need to take this very seriously indeed. You will need to find out why your child is avoiding school and work with the school on tackling the problem.

Building confidence: working with your child's teacher

If you are seriously concerned about your child's confidence or something which may be affecting it, then make an appointment to see your child's teacher – it is not something which can be discussed with her in five minutes at the end of the day.

Write down your thoughts and concerns before the meeting, but be careful not to start by accusing the teacher of not responding correctly to your child. Do not use phrases like 'What are you going to do about . . .' or 'You really ought to be . . .' Tell the teacher that you are concerned and want to help. Ask her for her opinion and make sure that she is aware of how your child's confidence has fallen. The teacher may need time to absorb the problem and work out some strategies to help. Ask if it would be appropriate to have a follow-up meeting when she has had time to think more about it.

Of course, the teacher may inform you about your child's lack of confidence in school when she has seemed fine at home. Do not dismiss this as being due to some children behaving differently at school or their confidence being affected by difficult situations. Even if there is something in the school environment which is affecting your child's confidence, talking about it at home will help.

Parents say . . .

> *I found talking to other parents invaluable. I really panicked when Rebecca came home upset whenever she had had an argument with a friend. Sometimes she wouldn't want to go to school the next day. Other mums reported the same problem – I guess all girls have to learn to get on and this takes time. Once I told Rebecca that all girls fall out sometimes and was even able to give her examples, she seemed to cope better. Mums of older girls also reassured me that it does get better – eventually!*

(Mother of Rebecca, 11)

> *I hated school and I was determined that Jack was going to like it. I emphasised all the painting and singing he would be doing and how he would make friends and play football. In fact, his favourite subject is maths! Schools are much more friendly and relaxed these days – I needn't have worried so much.*

(Mother of Jack, 9 and Sarah, 4)

> *Robbie has dyslexia and this meant being taken out of the class for special lessons. Before dyslexia was diagnosed, his life was miserable – now he has an answer to anyone who teases him – he gives them a great long list of famous and clever dyslexics like Einstein and Leonardo da Vinci.*

(Father of Robbie, 12)

'I found it very difficult when Hannah started school. Suddenly the house was empty and I would be waiting for her to come home. I would then get angry because she was tired and did not feel like giving me a blow-by-blow account of the day. In fact, I convinced myself that she must be unhappy. I gradually realised that it was me that had the problem. I went back to work part time and now have Hannah's 'problems' in perspective and don't go into a mega-panic whenever she's just tired or fed-up.'

(Mother of Hannah, 6)

'My twelve-year-old was bullied by a group of older girls. I wish I had done something about it sooner as we ended up sending her to a different school so that she could make a fresh start. It took her a long time to get her confidence back and I'm sure she would have been less affected if I'd noticed the signs earlier. I advise any parents to take school refusal or weepiness very seriously indeed. I treated my daughter as if she was being naughty because that's what it seemed like at the time.'

(Mother of two teenagers)

DOES YOUR CHILD HAVE A POSITIVE ATTITUDE TO SCHOOL ACHIEVEMENTS?

- Is your child self-motivated or do you have to really nag her to do her homework?
- Is your child conscientious or does she forget to do work or else not seem to care if it gets done or not?

- Does your child have an ambition for the future, seeing herself doing an interesting job at some time?
- Does your child go to school happily or does she try to avoid school whenever the opportunity arises?
- Is there at least one subject which your child positively enjoys?
- Does your child try to get the best marks that she can?
- Does your child get involved in after-school or lunch-time activities or does she only take part in what she really has to?
- Does your child mainly use her time well or is she always just 'hanging around'?
- Does your child look forward to going back to school after the holidays?
- Does your child check her appearance before she goes off to school in the mornings?

If you answered 'Yes' to the above questions or first part of the questions, then your child has such a positive attitude that you can leave her to get on with it, with your continuous encouragement of course. Some 'No's are inevitable and indicate that your child needs increased encouragement from you. Your child needs confidence and self-motivation to help her have a positive attitude to school. You can only nag so much – eventually it has got to come from her. The best that you can do is to be positive yourself and to build confidence in your child whenever you can. Encouragement and praise work better than nagging in the long term and working together with teachers can help to iron out any problems early on.

CHAPTER EIGHT

The teenage years

There needs to be a whole chapter dealing with teenagers as this is a vulnerable stage for losing confidence and self-esteem. It can also be one of the most challenging times for parents. They, too, can loose confidence when old tried and tested methods of parenting suddenly have to be abandoned to accommodate the changing needs of someone who is nearly adult and having to cope with the inevitable changes this brings.

It is these changes which can affect the self-esteem of even the most confident child. A combination of the physical and emotional changes of adolescence and the changes of lifestyle and expectations which occur as the end of school approaches will inevitably lead to some difficulties.

Knowing what to expect as well as how to deal with the common problems of adolescence can help parents to approach the teenage years with some confidence. But it is all too easy to expect the worst and approach this time with pessimism and even fear. Remember, it is not all bad and many parents get a great deal of pleasure from watching their young children transform into young adults. And with the right approach, your children can grow into *confident* young adults.

Problems which affect confidence

Mood swings

Teenagers can be very moody, which can confuse themselves as well as their parents. It is quite normal for a teenager to be quiet and withdrawn one day and boisterous and excitable the next. Moods can change suddenly and be very unpredictable. This can lead to a lack of confidence as inevitably there will be times when new situations have to be dealt with or new challenges met on just one of these moody days. Moodiness can affect relationships and can be the cause of making wrong decisions or just 'things going wrong'.

How to help

Make sure your teenager has his own private space where he can be 'moody' all on his own. When your teenager is in a calm mood, talk about the difficulties of these mood swings to show you understand. (These are rarely worth discussing at the time of the 'bad mood'.) Do not always assume that withdrawn behaviour is just a teenage mood caused by hormonal changes. There may be something specific worrying your child which he needs to talk about. Do encourage your teenager to talk about his feelings. He is more likely to try to control them if he is aware of them. However, do not expect total self-control during the adolescent years. Do remember to try to keep calm yourself.

Physical changes

If a teenager feels different in any way, it will affect his confidence and self-esteem. Many teenagers find the sudden physical changes very difficult to cope with and become very self-conscious. Because they are suddenly different physically from what they were before, they can conclude that somehow they are different from other people. Any changes which your child is unprepared for can also affect self-confidence; so a girl starting her periods without knowing the full facts or a teenager having sexual feelings without having talked about them can feel very alone and unsure.

How to help

Make sure that your child knows all about the physical and sexual changes which will take place. Tell him well in advance, not just once but many times over several years. This is an ongoing discussion, not a 'Sit down and I'll tell you the facts of life' discussion. Remind your teenager that you and your partner have been through it all too. Talk about how you felt at that time. Make sure that you emphasise that *all* teenagers have periods, sexual feelings, spots, voice changes or whatever. If you cannot talk about puberty and sex openly and frankly, then you may need help to combat your own inhibitions first. If you show embarrassment, then your teenager is not very likely to come to you with questions and problems. It often helps to buy your teenager a book about the physical changes. The more knowledge he has, the more in control he will feel.

Relationship difficulties

It is a normal part of development for teenagers to gain more of an interest in the opposite sex during the teenage years. A sexual interest is inevitable but teenagers develop both emotionally and physically at different rates, so physical relationships will start at different times for different teenagers. A lack of confidence can grow from the uncertainty of what friends of the opposite sex want. Teenagers who do not have opposite sex siblings or who are educated in single sex schools are very prone to have a lack of confidence when dealing with the opposite sex. Starting to have girlfriends and boyfriends can involve experiencing rejection which, of course, can take its toll on confidence.

How to help

Worries about appearance are often related to a wish to form relationships with the opposite sex. Boost your child's confidence by telling him when he looks good. Encourage your child to talk to you about his worries and fears about forming relationships. Make sure that your teenager has plenty of opportunities to mix with members of the opposite sex socially so that they can be regarded as friends rather than a species from another planet.

Try to accept that your child is no longer your baby. A first boyfriend or girlfriend can be a shock to parents who do not want their child to grow up quickly. Welcome friends of both sexes into your home, and let your child decide when he or she is old enough to have a girlfriend/boyfriend. Accept that your teenager will have sexual feelings but discuss the problem of peer pressure and of having sex before he is ready. At some point you may need to accept that your teenager is sexually active and discuss contraception.

Never pretend to yourself that your child is far too sensible to have sex in his teenage years. The majority do, but research has shown that those who can talk openly about sex to their parents and who have the knowledge are more likely to delay first sexual experiences than those who have not discussed it. Never threaten your child. Threats such as 'If I ever find out that you're . . .' will bolt the door of communication completely.

Feeling different

It is easy to think that teenagers want to be different, especially if they seem to stop conforming. But the fact is that teenagers who no longer conform to what parents or society want are usually conforming to their peer group. Look at any group of teenagers and you will note that they often dress alike and have the same sort of hair styles. Teenagers need to be accepted by their peer group and at the same time may break away from your values as they start to work out their own. For some teenagers, this may involve accepting that they do have differences from their peers or from what society expects. Some teenagers may come to realise that they have a different sexual orientation, for example. Feeling different can affect confidence.

How to help

Try not to have any pre-conceived ideas about what you expect your child to be like. Your child may change quite a lot during the teenage years. Before condemning any differences, try to see things from your teenager's point of view. He does not want to be different and may need help coming to terms with any differences as they occur. If your teenager thinks he may be gay, then listen. Help him to get some counselling which will help clarify the situation. He may be going through a normal stage of having a 'crush' on a member of the same 22
sex or he may indeed be gay. You may find that you also need counselling to help you accept and support your child whatever his sexuality.

How to keep your own confidence

- Accept that your child is growing up and that your role will gradually change.
- Accept that some of his opinions may be different from yours – he may join a different religion from you or become a vegetarian when you are not.
- Let your child make more of his own decisions but be there to help him make them.
- Teenagers still need rules and boundaries but it is even more important that they are involved in setting them and agree to a 'punishment' when they are broken.
- Make sure that you have a life of your own – a teenager still needs you but will spend more and more time away from your company.
- Never try to live your own ambitions out in your child – he will have his own.

- Do not be disappointed if he does not follow the course in life which you wanted him to. You may let your disappointment show, which will affect his confidence.
- Do not try to be the perfect parent. With teenagers, there will be times when you just cannot get it right.
- Spend time with other parents of teenagers. You are all in the same boat and talking together helps.

Coping with independence and decision making

A confident teenager should cope well with increased independence and with the important decisions which need to be made. However, very few teenagers are confident all the time and most will be affected by mood swings. You therefore have an important role to play in helping your child cope with the challenges of becoming an adult.

Your child is really 'in limbo' – no longer a child and yet not quite an adult. Looking ahead at the increased responsibility which adulthood brings can frighten some teenagers – so much so that they sometimes even 'drop out'. However, helping your teenager is not always easy – one minute he will seem to rely on your advice and help and the next minute he will want to do it all himself and seem to resent any interference from you. You therefore need to let your child take the lead.

Make sure that your teenager knows that you are always there to listen to him and make yourself approachable. You then need to leave it to him to approach you. However, if your child seems anxious or depressed, you will want to let him know that you know he's worried and, again, make it clear that you are there to help and not judge. Show him a strategy which may help him to make decisions. This could involve writing down all his thoughts on a subject as they come into his head, and then putting them in order of importance (the most important to him are usually those written down first) and dividing them into advantages and disadvantages. Make it clear that you do not want to make his decisions for him but that you can help him to get his thoughts into order. If you become too emotional or cannot keep your strong opinions back, then help your teenager to find someone else to talk it through with.

Try to make any increase in independence a gradual one, and make sure that you are slowly preparing your child for a life on his own. No teenager should leave home having never cooked a meal or ironed a shirt! Remember that you can no longer impose your decisions on your child once he is in his late teens. A discussion about drinking alcohol, perhaps coming to the conclusion that one or two drinks is enough, would be more effective than a straight 'You will not drink alcohol.'

The pressures of being a teenager

The teenage years can bring their own pressures which are bound to affect confidence from time to time. There are the pressures of the first important exams as well as the pressures of making important decisions about the future. At the same time, spending more time in the company of friends can bring its own pressures. Suddenly there's no longer a mum or dad to say 'Don't drink or take drugs' but a lot of other teenagers saying 'Do'. Suddenly the sex education learnt in the school room becomes a reality with a boyfriend putting pressure on your teenager to do what she may not feel ready to do.

As a parent with a mortgage or rent to pay and a demanding job to keep down, it is all too easy to look at your teenager and think that life must be easy. Parents can even get nostalgic about the teenage years when life seemed to be carefree and without pressures. But there are pressures and life certainly is not all easy-going for today's teenager. It probably never was – nostalgia has a funny way of making us forget the bad times!

How to help

- Acknowledge the difficulties that your teenager faces and try to show that you understand.
- Give practical help – a quiet place to study and a family pact to leave your teenager in peace to study at certain times.
- Always be available to listen and never brush any problem aside as trivial.
- Help to boost your child's confidence in times of pressure.
- Encourage your child to succeed and not to have unrealistically high expectations.
- Do set boundaries but discuss them with your teenager first. Too many 'Thou shalt nots' rarely work.

Coping with success and failure

During the teenage years, your child will inevitably experience successes and failures. Failure without success can understandably affect confidence and yet it would be a rare teenager who managed to avoid failure altogether. Even those teenagers who do well in tests and exams may experience a failed relationship or a loss in a sport or hobby. Your child therefore needs to be able to cope with failures and disappointments if he is to keep his confidence intact.

How to help

Establish whether your child really has failed or if he just has very high expectations. You may need to help your child set realistic goals (see below). If your child consistently fails at one thing in life, get him to make a chart of his strengths and weaknesses. Make sure that there are more strengths. Set goals to help him overcome his weaknesses. Your child needs to accept that he cannot be perfect at everything. Emphasise his successes and make sure his aims are realistic.

Give your child a cooling-off period following a failure. Of course he does not want to talk about re-sitting an exam straight after a failure or going to another job interview straight after a rejection. Try not to focus your own life one hundred per cent on your children. If they sense that your dreams are to be met in them, this unconsciously puts pressure on them to succeed and any failure will be edged with a sense of letting you down. Show that you understand how disappointed your child is at a time of failure. This is a time of sympathy rather than wallowing in your own disappointment. If your child feels that he has let you down too, this will make him feel more of a failure and will make it difficult for him to discuss it with you.

Helping your child to set goals

Goal setting can be useful at any age but really comes into its own during the teenage years. Before this, it tends to be useful for dealing with a particular problem or difficulty, but in general can put pressure on a younger child or restrict his spontaneity and creativity.

Setting goals can directly help your teenager's confidence. First of all, get your child to set goals in small steps so as to reduce any feelings of failure. This will give your child a feeling of being in control and will help him to feel motivated and positive. And of course, once the goal has been achieved, the success will boost your child's confidence no end.

Goals must be . . .

- Set by your child or in total agreement with your child.
- Realistic.
- Broken down into smaller goals.
- Flexible and changeable if necessary.
- Rewarding when they are met. You could even set a specific reward with your teenager, such as a treat out when he achieves his goal.

- Put in order of priority if there is more than one goal.
- Specific. A goal of 'doing my best at school' is too vague. A goal of 'getting my homework done on time' is more specific.
- Short or long term – but long-term goals can be broken down into several short-term goals.
- Accompanied by a plan of action. A goal of 'getting my homework done on time' may include a timetable of when to study.

Direct action on confidence

When confidence seems low, you may want to take more direct action. All the general information about boosting confidence outlined earlier in this book still applies, for example telling your teenager that you like him or that he looks nice. It is all too easy to forget to do this as your teenager grows up and demands less of your time, especially if you do not get much of a response now. Your toddler may have thrown his arms around you and given you a big hug when you told him how much you liked him. Now, he just shrugs his shoulders. But still say it – it is going in. Confidence may be affected by very specific things at this age such as appearance – perhaps acne has spoilt the confidence of a child who was used to being admired – and teenage pressures. Boost your teenager's confidence in the additional ways given below.

Give practical help with appearance

This does not mean telling your teenager what to wear or how to have his hair. However, you might suggest practical treatment for spots or greasy hair. Or you might suggest wearing less outrageous clothes for, say, a job interview. There is no need to criticise him when you do this, just point out that some employers judge by appearance and it is worth looking the part.

Tell your teenager when his face or hair looks better and praise any effort he makes for formal occasions. Accept that appearance is important to him while making sure that his apparent obsession with appearance does not get out of hand. Praise him for his other qualities so that not everything is focused on looks.

Role play difficult situations

When a difficult situation approaches, preparation can help your teenager feel more confident. Part of this preparation can include role play. For example, if your teenager has a job interview approaching, you can ask some likely questions so that he can practise his answers. Role play it properly so that you sit in a typical interview set-up, perhaps opposite your child. You could even get a friend who he does not know very well to take the part of the interviewer. Working out what to ask in advance when looking around a college or new school can help when a lack of confidence is likely to render your teenager speechless. In fact, any difficult situation can be role played, but if your teenager finds this difficult with you, then an assertiveness course may help. These usually incorporate role play into their programmes.

Put it in writing

Get your teenager to list his strengths and weaknesses. Many a teenager lacking in confidence will end up with a list of weaknesses, many based on appearance. You can help to build up the list of strengths and then help to deal with any weaknesses in a practical way. You can also turn any weaknesses into strengths by wording them in a more positive way. For example, if your teenager has a weakness of 'not being able to talk easily with people', point out that he is a good listener. And if your teenager lists greasy hair as a weakness, point out that the colour and style are a strength.

Give your teenager more trust and responsibility

One of the best ways of boosting your child's confidence is to show him that he can do it for himself and that you trust him to do it. Responsibility should be increased gradually over the teenage years so that he is not 'thrown in at the deep end'. The aim, of course, is that when your teenager leaves home, he can look after himself and has had plenty of practice with all that this involves. So, let your teenager have friends to stay the night provided he gets the evening meal or breakfast and cleans up afterwards. Or let your teenager borrow your clothes providing she washes and irons them afterwards. Trust your teenager to go out in the evenings provided he sticks to the rules of being in at an appointed time. Or you may trust your teenager to go camping with friends provided he sticks to the rules such as phoning you at set times. Praise him for being independent and responsible but explain that independence will be taken away if responsibility is abused.

Activities for confidence

Your teenager will cope with the challenges that independence and responsibility bring if they come gradually. Group activities supervised by other adults can enable your teenager to take the first steps away from you without knocking his confidence or turning you into an over-anxious parent.

Holidays Accept that your teenager will eventually prefer to have holidays with friends rather than family. Try to have a positive view of this yourself – perhaps you and your partner can enjoy a holiday alone for the first time in years. A first holiday away from parents can be an organised activity holiday for teenagers. The British Activity Holiday Association (address at the back of the book) lists organisations which have such holidays available. This will give you peace of mind and your teenager the feeling of independence he needs.

Clubs Youth clubs or clubs revolving around a particular sport or interest can also help with confidence. Your teenager has the opportunity to talk to others in a familiar setting, to deal with success and failure and even to take on some position of responsibility. Clubs and societies also enable your teenager to spend evenings or weekends away from the family and may even involve longer periods away.

Parents say . . .

> *One minute Jonathon is like a child and the next minute like a young adult. This makes being a parent very difficult as you feel you have to change to suit their moods. I find the worst thing that you can do is try to hang on to those times when they need you most. They have to grow up and as parents we have to let them.*
>
> *(Mother of Jonathon, 14)*

> *Having a teenager makes you re-evaluate your own views on things. My son gave such good reasons for wanting to be a vegetarian that he made us all think again. Now the whole family have gone vegetarian. I feel sorry for the families who put such things down as a teenage fad. Teenagers are intelligent beings who do think things out for themselves. We have to accept that they will not always agree with our views on things.*
>
> *(Mother of Michael, 13)*

> *I think we all approach the teenage years with fear and dread. It has not been as bad as I thought. The worst thing has been Hyacinth's moods. At first, I would do anything to try to talk her out of it but I*

soon realised that all she needed was to be on her own. Now I just send her out with the dog and by the time she comes back, it's all over. And if it isn't then so what? She bounces back eventually. ’

(Mother of Hyacinth, 12)

‘ *If they are going to try drugs or sex, then they will whether you drag them in at 10.30 p.m. or let them stay out longer. We cannot follow them around twenty-four hours a day so we have to let go and trust them. All you can really do is keep your fingers crossed and talk openly about the problems they are likely to come up against.* ’

(Mother of Gareth, 15 and Hamish, 16)

‘ *It seems unfair that just when you hit the menopause, your children hit the teenage years. We have enough hormonal imbalance in our family to tip the house over. It should help us understand each other more – but in reality it can get quite fraught. How do I cope? Well, I give them lots of space and privacy and encourage my partner to deal with problems when I just feel too fraught to deal with them myself.* ’

(Mother of three teenage girls)

Will your teenager grow into a confident adult?

1 Your teenager starts going out to parties in the evenings and getting back later and later. Do you:

a Leave things as they are – he is old enough to make his own decisions?
b Sit down together and agree on a time for coming in and any other ground rules such as not walking home alone?
c Set a time for him based on what other parents say?

2 Your teenager breaks the rule of what time to come in and comes in an hour late. Do you:

a Tell him not to do it again?
b Find out why he is late and impose a previously agreed punishment (perhaps grounding) if there is no good reason?
c Change the home-coming time to an hour earlier?

3 You think the other teenager your child is hanging around with is a bad influence. Do you:

a Let him choose his own friends and not interfere?
b Invite the friend home to get to know him better. Only commenting if there is something specific which the friend has done?
c Ban your child from seeing his new friend?

4 Your teenager goes to school looking like an extra from 'Oliver'. Do you:

a Let him wear what he likes without comment?
b Sit down to decide when your child can wear what he chooses and when it might be better to choose something more conventional?
c Throw the clothes away and make him wear something more sensible?

5 You think your sixteen-year-old may be having a sexual relationship with his girlfriend. Do you:

a Say nothing as he is old enough to know his own mind?
b Sit down and talk to him about what he really wants from his relationship, advising on contraception if necessary?
c Confront him and ground him if necessary?

6 Your teenager decides he no longer wants to go on to further education but would like to join a pressure group and get things changed. Do you:

a Not interfere and let him live his own life?
b Sit down to talk about the advantages and disadvantages of such a decision? Talk about other options such as doing both or taking a year out before college?
c Tell your child to pull himself together?

7 Your teenager has become very withdrawn and no longer seems to mix. Do you:

a Leave him alone as interfering only makes it worse?
b Talk to him to find out if there is anything wrong? Encourage him to invite friends round as a step forward?
c Take him to the local youth club and tell him to enjoy himself?

You will realise that the answers for confidence are the *b*s – your teenager needs guidance from you and someone to talk to. However, he also needs to feel that his views are important and that he plays a part in making decisions. The *c* answers suggest trying to control a teenager's life too much. Not allowing a teenager to make decisions or to take on any responsibility will not build confidence, and when your child has to cope alone, his confidence will be severely affected. The *a* answers allow your teenager too much freedom. They may be suitable for an older, mature teenager but most teenagers still need some guidance. Left with no rules or guidelines, a teenager can actually lose confidence. Confidence comes from knowing what is expected of ourselves and during the teenage years, parents can help outline these expectations.

CHAPTER NINE

Getting help

So far, this book has mainly considered how to help your own child gain confidence and how you can deal with the problems which affect confidence by yourself. However, there may be occasions when you need to consider getting outside help or advice. In very difficult cases, this may involve a referral to a relevant professional for treatment or counselling. Other circumstances may indicate that a self-help group would help. Getting outside help can be a difficult decision to make. It usually involves acknowledging that a problem has got too big for you to deal with and may mean taking a very direct line with your child. Understandably, you may not want to make a 'big thing' of your child's problems and, by involving professionals, you will seem to be doing just that. For older children and teenagers, it is important that they are aware of any referral and hopefully agree to see the professional involved.

When should you get help?

- When your child has asked for the sort of help which you can not provide.
- When your child has a very specific problem which may result from a lack of confidence. This could be anything from truancy to anorexia.

- When your child has a very specific problem which affects confidence. This could be anything from a stammer to a facial deformity.
- When your child would clearly benefit from meeting other children with the same problem.
- When you acknowledge that you do not know enough about the problem yourself.
- When you, as a parent, need help and advice on how to deal with your child's problem.

When you should delay getting help

- Do not be impulsive and get help out of a sudden panic. Discuss it with your partner or perhaps your child's teacher first.
- It is better to get your child's agreement first. Firstly, she may need help with acknowledging that she does have a problem.
- There may be an enforced delay if there is a waiting list for the help you need. Do get your child referred – you can always change your mind if things get better in the meantime.
- If you are already making progress and you feel you can cope without help. You can, of course, get advice yourself without involving your child.

Help for parents

Self-help groups Discussing your child's confidence with a group of parents can help in two main ways. Firstly, you will realise that the problems you and your child are experiencing are shared by others. Secondly, you can share practical ideas to help each other. It also helps to get your thoughts in perspective just to discuss the problem. Contact 'Exploring Parenthood' or 'Parent Network/Parent-Link' who may have a branch in your area (details at the back of the book).

Support agencies You may just want one experienced counsellor or supporter to talk to. Contact 'Home-Start' (details at the back of the book) who send in a helper-parent to talk to (under fives only).
Specific support groups There are support groups for your individual circumstances. 'Stepfamily' or 'Gingerbread' for single-parent families, for example (details at the back of the book).
Relationship support Your child's lack of confidence may result from your relationship problems. Contact 'Relate' (details at the back of the book).

Low-key help for your child

Indirect self-help groups

Some activity groups may help your child with confidence almost as a by-product of the activity. The obvious example is a drama group, although any activity group can help with social skills or even leadership skills. Your child must have a positive view of the group. It is better for her to join an activity which she is interested in rather than be dragged reluctantly to drama or elocution. You may consider this type of group before making a more formal application for a self-help group which is more directly involved in building confidence.

Direct self-help groups

Older children can benefit from an assertiveness course and details can be found at your local library or citizen's advice bureau. Or you can contact the 'Self-Esteem Network' (details at the back of the book) who may be able to advise on suitable courses.

Your child may need a self-help group to help with a particular problem which is contributing to low self-esteem. For example, the Association for Stammering can give you details of a suitable self-help group in your area. There are too many possibilities to list here but do contact your citizens advice bureau for information about your child's particular problem.

Professional help for your child

Child and family psychiatry/family therapy

Sadly, there is a great stigma attached to psychiatry and yet psychiatrists can help give you enormous insight into your child's problems. They do not just treat people who are severely mentally ill but can advise on all types of behaviour problems too.

The tendency now is to look at the family as a whole and you will all be expected to attend. Some family therapy sessions are conducted by a clinical psychologist, sometimes a child psychiatrist and sometimes both. In fact, a whole team may be involved and as parents you form part of that team – your input is invaluable. The difference between a child psychiatrist and a clinical psychologist is one of training. A child psychiatrist is a doctor with specialist training whereas a clinical or child psychologist has a psychology degree and has done further training in behaviour and child development. You will need to see your GP for a referral. Most clinics are based in a hospital.

Educational psychologist

If your child has learning difficulties or problems at school then an educational psychologist can help. Perhaps your child's confidence has been affected by poor school achievements or specific learning difficulties. Your school can refer your child to an educational psychologist or your doctor or health visitor can refer a preschool child. Educational psychologists are trained first in teaching and then in psychology. They are experts in child development and are able to carry out IQ tests and developmental assessments.

Child psychotherapist

A referral from your GP is necessary for a child psychotherapist who is concerned with the treatment of deep-rooted emotional difficulties.

Health visitors

Anxiety about your child's development can affect both your own confidence and your child's. Health visitors are trained nurses with a further training in child development. They can give you initial advice on dealing with normal behaviour patterns such as temper tantrums or bed wetting. They will support the whole family at times of stress and are able to refer you on to other professionals where necessary. They are also a useful source of practical information such as where the nearest playgroups or childminders are.

Social worker

Social workers become involved with any families who may have problems. Again, they are a good source of information and can refer you to other professionals where necessary.

Counsellor

Your GP may be able to refer you or your child to a counsellor who may be a social worker with additional training. Counsellors are trained to understand and advise on educational, emotional and personal matters. Some GP practices have their own counsellor. Some agencies have counsellors for specific things, such as 'Cruse' who provide bereavement counsellors. For older children, a counsellor may be available through the school. Beware of private counsellors who advertise, as anyone can call themselves a counsellor. It is best to get a GP referral. The essence of counselling is to help you to make decisions or to come to terms with a difficulty. A good counsellor will listen but will not make the decisions for you.

Alternative help

Complementary or alternative therapies can help with confidence. You will not need a referral from a GP but will need to contact the therapist yourself. You will generally pay for private treatments and therapies, although there are sometimes self-help groups based around an alternative approach.

Hypnotherapy

This begins with the therapist guiding the client into a hypnotic state through using relaxation, imagery or visualisation. The client can visualise her problems away and some hypnotherapists claim that confidence can be increased and fears eliminated. Check out the therapist's qualifications with the The British Register of Complementary Practitioners (Hypnotherapy section) – details at the back of the book. There is a recent trend for trained psychotherapists and doctors to take further training in hypnosis techniques.

Autogenic training

This is a form of self-hypnosis which can help the user feel positive, perhaps about a particular situation. It also helps to relieve stress and is good for relaxation. Contact the British Association for Autogenic Training and Therapy (address at the back of the book) for details of a practitioner in your area. Ultimately, the practitioner will teach you to do this for yourself.

Drama therapy, dance therapy and art therapy

These encourage you to express emotions through the medium of dance, art or drama. They deal more directly with self-esteem than just joining a dance, drama or art club. Drama therapy, for example, will deal with relating to others, coping with difficult situations through role play, and handling emotions. (Useful addresses at the back of the book.)

Relaxation and stress relief techniques

Children lacking in confidence or self-esteem often find it difficult to relax. Difficult situations make them tense which, in turn, affects confident behaviour. There are many types of relaxation therapies which can help. Aromatherapy and massage can induce relaxation, while yoga and meditation techniques can be taught so that your child can use them when and how she chooses. (Useful addresses at the back of the book.)

Specific help

There are many things which affect self-confidence which can be helped by support and treatment. Wherever possible, consider what the cause of low confidence is and tackle the cause rather than the symptoms. In some cases, the cause of low confidence is obvious, although part of the treatment may be to accept the difficulty or disability rather than cure it. You will almost certainly want to seek professional help for the following problems.

Communication difficulties

Other children are bound to comment if your child has a speech difficulty such as a lisp or a stammer. Your child may become very self-conscious and may be reluctant to communicate. Ask your GP, health visitor or school for a referral to a speech and language therapist. Tell the therapist how the problem is affecting your child's behaviour.

Appearance

Your child may be self-conscious about looking different and in some cases this can be helped by medical treatment and/or counselling. 'Let's Face It' or the Naevus Support Group can help with facial disfigurements or birthmarks (addresses at the back of the book).

Intelligence

This could involve a child with learning difficulties or a very gifted child. Either way, your child will feel different. Being highly intelligent can affect confidence, especially as gifted children are very susceptible to bullying. If your child is struggling at school, ask the head teacher to refer her to an educational psychologist who may recommend further specialist help. If your child is gifted but finding this difficult to cope with, contact the National Association for Gifted Children (address at the back of the book) as well as discussing it with her teacher.

Eating problems

Children with eating disorders such as anorexia nervosa usually have very poor self-esteem and give themselves no value at all. These disorders need specialist help and counselling. See your GP or contact the Eating Disorders Association (address at the back of the book).

Drug use

A lack of confidence can help to lead your child to joining in with the pack rather than sticking to her own beliefs. Alternatively a child lacking in confidence may try to boost confidence with drugs or alcohol. You will need to talk to your child in a non-judgmental way in order to persuade her to get specialist help. You can get appropriate help and counselling through your GP.

School phobia, bullying and truancy

Work with the school to find out the reasons behind these problems. If your child has been bullied, she will need help to get her confidence back and some techniques to help her know what to say if it happens again. The charity 'Kidscape' (address at the back of the book) can give advice on this. It may be that your child is doing the bullying herself and, although this cannot be condoned, it does need approaching with some understanding. A bullier often lacks confidence herself and is trying to gain control of her life by controlling other children. Perhaps she has difficulty making friends or being accepted. A bullier is often very unhappy and needs as much help as the victim. A child avoiding school through truancy or pretending to be ill could be a victim of bullying, or perhaps she is failing at school. A meeting with staff at the school is essential as well as a non-judgmental chat with your child to find out what the problem is.

Depression

Depression in very young children is very rare and when it does occur is likely to be linked to a specific traumatic event. However, teenagers are quite likely to go through depressive phases. Adolescents are very volatile and can be happy and optimistic one day and irritable or even depressed the next. With understanding and support, most teenagers get through these 'down' periods fairly quickly. A few may show more serious signs of continued depression which could require outside help. The warning signs are:

- A persistent feeling of depression (rather than the normal adolescent mood swings).
- Difficulty leading a normal life – perhaps some activities including friendships are dropped completely.
- Neglect of personal hygiene and appearance.
- Not eating properly.
- Not sleeping properly.
- Bad school performance.
- Lack of concentration.

If your teenager seems seriously depressed, contact your GP. He may then refer your teenager on to another professional for counselling. Alternatively, you could contact the school who may provide a counselling service themselves. At any rate, staff will be alerted to the problem and can keep a close eye on your daughter or son.

Family problems

Confidence can be affected by sudden changes in the family. Perhaps your child feels she has to compete with a new step-parent or step-brothers and sisters. A change in routine or a feeling of uncertainty when changes occur is bound to affect confidence for a while. By looking at the situation from your child's point of view, you may be able to provide enough understanding and support to ensure that changes happen as smoothly as possible and without too many long-term effects on your child. However, both you and your child may benefit from talking to an outsider or just by getting advice from an appropriate organisation. Contact 'Gingerbread' for support if you become a one-parent family or the National Stepfamily Association who run a helpline (details of both are given at the end of the book). If your family is affected by a bereavement, then 'CRUSE' (bereavement care) may help. CRUSE has counsellors who specialise in talking to children and recommend useful books and leaflets.

Criminal behaviour

It is very shocking to discover that your child is involved in criminal behaviour, such as shop-lifting or vandalism. It may be that your child has lacked the confidence to state her own views when in a group of children and has just 'gone with the pack'. A child may be put off this activity for good just by getting a warning from the police or else getting into serious trouble at school. Although you will not want to condone the behaviour, you should try to talk calmly to your child to find out why and how it happened. If your child persistently commits petty crimes, do get help. A child psychologist may be able to help and your GP can make the necessary referral.

Children who indulge in petty crime often have difficulty dealing with authority – they are often aggressive towards those in charge and rebel against both parents and teachers. Do get advice from parenting organisations such as 'Parentline' or 'Parent Network' on how to discipline children without being too authoritarian.

Consulting the expert: what to expect

Once your child has been referred to an expert – perhaps a child psychologist – you may have to wait. Ask your GP what the likely waiting time is. You may want to telephone the relevant department to indicate that you are prepared to take a cancelled appointment at short notice. If there is a long wait for an appointment, do carry on tackling the problem or handling it as best you can. Do not stop your own efforts as if the appointment is immediately going to solve everything.

Find out as much about what to expect at the appointment as you can so that you can be prepared and can prepare your child. In most cases, you can expect to see a multi-disciplinary team, sometimes all together and sometimes separately. Do not have a big build up, or even a count down, days before the appointment, making your child feel that it is the most important thing that has ever happened. Equally, do not make her feel that now all her problems will be resolved in one easy session. Let her know when and where you are going and leave it at that until the day itself. Make sure she is busy on the appointment day, not just hanging around waiting for it to happen. It is a good idea to write down what you particularly want to say before the visit, as your mind can easily go blank in a stressful or new situation. If your child is older, get her to write down anything she wants to say too.

Try to get your child to relax before the appointment. Do not arrive so early that you have a long time to tense up and get worried, but do not let yourselves feel rushed either. You should all take something to look at in the waiting room in an attempt to relax. The professionals involved will do their best to help you feel at ease and to explain everything that is happening. Do ask if there is anything you do not fully understand.

Let your child relax after the appointment and when she is ready talk to her about it. Make sure that she has understood everything that has been said and find out how she feels about the session. If you are not satisfied with the appointment, do give it another try if further sessions are recommended. Ask your GP if you wish to have another opinion from a different expert.

Home help

It may be that you want to take a very direct approach to helping your child with confidence or a confidence-linked problem but do not feel the need to involve an outside professional. Essentially, this book has been concerned with just that – how to help your child at home. You will already have considered how to parent for confidence and how to deal with the likely problems as they occur at each stage of development. However, you may want to be even more direct and consider the following methods.

- Seek the advice of experts without directly involving your child. This may involve telephoning information or help lines or it may mean making an appointment for yourself.
- Read books about the particular problem you are dealing with. A relevant organisation may have written information available or a recommended book list.
- Encourage your older child to read about a problem or even to read books about confidence and assertiveness.
- Start your own self-help group. You could place an advert in the paper to contact families with similar concerns to your own. For teenagers, you might aim ultimately to back off completely and let them run it themselves.

- Get the whole family involved in something which will help your child. For example, you could all join a self-defence group. Or perhaps you too lack assertiveness – so why not go along to a group with your child?
- Find something that each member of the family needs to work on. Perhaps you have one child who needs to be more confident in social situations so his aim could be to talk to someone new at the youth club every week. Find an aim for each family member – perhaps you need to give up eating chocolate or your partner needs to exercise three times a week. Now have a 'star chart' and think of a reward for yourselves once you have all reached your goals. This means that the child with low confidence does not feel singled out as having a problem. It also means you can all give each other encouragement and support.
- If you find it difficult to help your child or if she seems reluctant to talk to you, do consider involving another adult. Perhaps a grandparent or close family friend would be prepared to take on the role of confident. This does not mean that you are opting out. Once your child can confide in someone outside her immediate family, she may feel more ready to confide in you.
- Remember that you and your partner are the experts on your child. Make sure that discussions with your partner are constructive and not tense, fraught or always likely to lead to an argument. A time needs to be set aside for discussing serious concerns – and not as you are going out the door for work. Before you discuss a problem it may help if you each write your thoughts down for the other to read.
- Beware the amateur 'expert' who is keen to offer advice at the bus stop or in the supermarket checkout queue. Do listen to other parents who have experienced similar problems with their own children. Do not listen to well meaning do-gooders who simply have a very black and white view of what all children need.

Parents say. . .

It was the church that gave my son the confidence he needed. Joining the church youth club was very hard for him but he stuck at it and seems to make friends more easily now. The main thing is that he has read the lesson in church many times now and feels much more confident about standing up in front of a group of people.

(Mother of Jonathon, 14)

I was devastated when my son had to see an educational psychologist because of his behaviour at school and his poor performance. There is a stigma attached to seeing a psychologist but she was very positive and offered very practical help to both the school and ourselves. I had imagined she would criticise us or our child but no, it was positive and helpful.

(Father of Robbie, 12)

My husband and I both attended the Parent Link groups because we were having endless battles with our daughter. I think underneath we already knew how to handle her but sometimes you need to take a step back and think about what you are doing. Talking to other parents definitely helps.

(Mother of Samantha, 5 and Jeremy, 2)

'It was Kevin's teacher who first got us to realise that his lack of confidence was affecting him quite badly. And it was her that really helped him. She made his confidence something to work on and gave it the same importance as maths and spelling. She got him taking errands to other classrooms and helped him participate in news time, encouraging him to stand up and show things to the rest of the class.'

(Father of Kevin, 8)

Checklist: Does your child need help?

Get expert help if:

- Your child asks for it.
- You do not fully understand your child's problem.
- You or your child do not know other children/families with the same problem.
- You know you are handling it badly.
- Your child's teacher recommends outside help.
- You feel at the end of your tether.
- Your child feels at the end of her tether.
- The problem seems to have got out of hand.
- You and your child have difficulty talking about it.
- You want more information about the problem.
- Your child wants more information about the problem.
- The resulting tension and anxiety are affecting all aspects of your child's life.
- You and your child have found support from experts helpful in the past.
- Your child may be clinically depressed.

CHAPTER TEN

It's never too late

Whatever your child's age and whatever his problems have been in the past, it's never too late to give him the confidence he needs. However, you must remember that these things take time. A child with a poor self-image will need at least six months to turn that image into a positive one. The process is a gradual one and a parent must stick at the confidence-boosting regime for as long as it takes. You are bound to feel despondent at times and may even start to think that you are over-doing it, that your encouragement and praise sound somehow too obvious. Just try putting yourself in your child's shoes. How do you feel when someone takes the time to tell you you look nice or that you made a good job of something? Pretty good – and I doubt you would ever complain about being praised and appreciated too much! Here we consider some of the problems which you may encounter as your child grows. Remember, it is never too late to deal with your child's low confidence or poor self-esteem. And it is never too late to tackle the problems which can affect that confidence.

> ‘*My child is fairly confident but this all goes to pieces if there is a dog around. He will not go and play with someone who has a dog and screams whenever he sees one in the street.*’

Any phobia can affect confidence and needs to be tackled straightaway. Many phobias start with a particular incident – perhaps your child was frightened by an aggressive dog at some time. Any child can develop a phobia although nervous children are most at risk.

Your child needs to learn that many dogs can be friendly and this has to be learnt gradually. As with any fear, your child must learn to face it in very gradual stages indeed. In the case of a dog, you would start by looking at pictures and videos of dogs, talking positively about how friendly they can be. Next you need to find a friend with a very placid dog. Tell your child that you are going to look at it from across the street or through the window, promising that you won't be going any nearer. Let your child watch someone stroke the dog. Over a period of weeks, move nearer to the dog until your child is ready to stroke it. Gradually, your child will relearn how he feels about dogs and although he may not be a dog-lover for some time, it should make day-to-day living easier.

> ‘ *My five-year-old wets her bed whenever anything has gone wrong during the day. In the morning, she feels embarrassed and awkward.* ’

Firstly, remember that one in ten five-year-olds wet their beds occasionally. This fact may help you to feel less worried about the situation as your five-year-old will certainly react to any anxiety you have. Make sure that you have a quiet time at the end of the day for a story and a chat. This should include an opportunity for your child to talk about any worries she may have and for you to be understanding and reassuring. Make sure she uses the toilet before and after the story – going twice in quick succession makes wetting the bed less likely. If the bed is wet in the morning, do not over-react, just say 'Never mind, try again tonight.' Do not look upset or annoyed about it and do not get into a long conversation about it. Praise your child when she does have a dry night. You can even use a star chart.

> *My thirteen-year-old never confides in me. He even hides things from me including his rather poor school report.*

Your teenager is entitled to his privacy and can choose what he does and does not want to tell you. Do tell him that you respect his choice not to talk about everything and that you will not pry into any personal problems unless he wants you to. At the same time, you must let him know that you are there to listen when he does want to talk. Make sure you listen and give your sympathy and understanding where it is needed. There is often no need to be judgmental – instead you can ask your child what *he* thinks about the situation or about his behaviour.

As for the school report, it was probably addressed to you and you should therefore explain to your son that this is not a private matter just for him. Again, ask him what he feels about his school report and try not to be too judgmental until he has had a chance to talk about it. Make sure that you discuss it calmly – a shouting match will not do any good. He may feel very upset about the report and feel that you will be annoyed too. Try to focus on anything that is good in the report and tell him that he must be very disappointed. Do not show your own disappointment – instead try to work out some practical ideas for working on the subjects he finds most difficult.

> *My nine-year-old relies on my opinion for everything. If we go out to buy a new jumper, she wants the one that I choose for her.*

Limit her choice so that perhaps you pick out just two items for her to choose from. When she asks you what you think, do not rush in with your opinion but ask her what she thinks first. Perhaps your child is not used to making choices, so think about other day-to-day decisions she could be involved in such as choosing what to have for tea or even helping you to choose what to wear. Perhaps your child lacks confidence in making decisions because some of her ideas have not always been taken seriously. Ask your child's opinion about something at least once a day and show an interest in her ideas even if they are impractical.

> ‘*My child is over-sensitive to criticism and even teasing. You have to watch what you say the whole time in case he takes it the wrong way.*’

This is certainly an indication that basic confidence is lacking. You need to spend time praising your child and boosting his confidence in the ways outlined in this book. At the same time, you can get him used to receiving criticism and teasing. In fact, he should never receive direct criticism from you – when you do have to criticise you can mix it in with a certain amount of praise too. For example you might say ‘You tidied up the lounge so well yesterday, what a pity you left your bedroom in such a mess today.’ Or even ‘I think you forgot to tidy your bedroom but never mind, it's not too late – do you want to do it now or after tea?’

You can also get your child used to teasing by doing some gentle teasing in the family. Let him hear you tease an older sibling or your partner while they laugh it off. Talk to your child about teasing and explain how it can be fun and does not have to be unkind at all. Tell him you are going to tease him and then do it. Ask him how it felt. Once he can cope with this pre-warned teasing, tell him you are going to do some gentle teasing during the day. Encourage him to tease you and explain when teasing is fun and when it is unkind. In other words, you can de-sensitise your child to teasing so that he copes better when it happens outside the family.

> ‘*I always seem to be nagging my young children and telling them what to do. I don't want them to see me as a real old bag and I don't want to knock their natural confidence.*’

To start with try to work out what it is you nag your children about. If it is constant shouts of 'Mind the ornaments' then put the ornaments away and if you are constantly shouting 'Hang your coats up!' then make sure this is easy for them by having low coat hooks in an accessible place. In other words, try to create a nag-free environment. If you are nagging them about certain behaviour, then try to turn it into something positive by praising them when they do get it right. Perhaps you could have a star chart with a star earned every time they, say, remember to put their shoes away. Do not be worried about the occasional nag – young children need structured guidelines on how to behave – but make sure you do not nag more than you praise.

> *My teenager really lacks confidence when it comes to exams. He tenses up and goes to pieces. How can I help?*

Teach your child how to relax. You can do this by buying a relaxation tape or else you can teach him a progressive relaxation technique. To do this, he should sit or lie comfortably and then tense up one part of his body, say his foot. He should then relax it and feel the difference. He should do this for each part of his body and as each part is relaxed imagine it is getting heavier. Once relaxed, your child can take deep breaths from the diaphragm (the area near the stomach, not the chest) and let the breaths out slowly. He needs to practise relaxation so that by exam time he can do it effectively. Meanwhile he needs time and space to study.

Help him to plan his study – many students and school children waste a lot of time worrying about the studying they should be doing rather than getting on with it. A precise and realistic study plan should help. Set up little tests at home to get him used to the situation and get him to visualise himself in an exam, coping well. He also needs to feel positive, so remind him how well he has been doing in certain subjects. If possible, get him to have an evening off before an exam to relax and unwind. A certain amount of tension on the day is no bad thing – children do better if they are keyed up so long as it is not too much.

> *I dread the teenage years. I have always been good with small children but I have no confidence in how I will be as a parent when my children are teenagers.*

Luckily, our children do not turn into typical teenagers overnight – they grow into this stage gradually. You will probably have more confidence once they are there as you will have had a gradual build up. You must do two things – prepare yourself and be positive. To prepare yourself, talk to other parents who have teenagers or who have been right through the teenage years with their children and have come out the other side intact and happy. You can also read books on coping with teenagers which will focus your mind on the sort of challenges ahead. And do think of them as challenges and not problems. To be positive, write down all the things you think are good about having and being a teenager – perhaps you will enjoy the extra freedom it will bring you or perhaps you will enjoy having lively young people in the home. Not all teenagers drop out, take drugs or stay out all night, every night. In fact, most manage to get through this stage with very few problems other than the usual moodiness. So do not expect the worst, but be prepared for all eventualities.

> *Now my children are older, I cannot just give them rules and leave it at that. They challenge any rules I set, always begging to stay out just another hour or get let off the washing-up rota. I do not want to undermine their independence and therefore their confidence.*

Of course confidence does come from independence but if too much independence is introduced too quickly, then this can have the opposite effect. Your children still need the security of rules and regulations so they know where they stand and what is expected of them. And you still need rules for your own peace of mind, their safety and just for the ease of running a family unit. However, you have to move on from you setting the rules to the family setting them together. You are now looking for agreements, sometimes written and you will need all the skills of negotiation to get the necessary rules laid down.

To take the example of coming home times, you need to discuss this as a family. First get your children to agree that having a set time to be in is a good thing – do give rational explanations such as needing to know where they are for safety reasons, needing enough sleep before school and so on. Most children will agree to the principle of a set time. A good negotiator will set her sights above what she really wants. This gives you room for compromise and lets your children feel that you have given them some concessions. So if you are aiming for an 11.00 p.m. curfew, you might start by asking for 10.30 p.m. allowing them to negotiate the extra half hour in return for, say, having three nights at home to do homework. At the end of the discussion, both you and your children should feel that they have got a good deal.

Encourage your children to see things from your point of view, perhaps explaining that you cannot rest until they are in. At the same time, though, you must see things from your children's point of view. Make sure you write down any agreements and stick them up on the kitchen wall. This should include any agreed punishments, such as grounding, if rules are broken without a good reason. Do prepare yourself with the facts before any discussion about rules. Your children are bound to list others who are treated differently from them by perhaps being allowed out later. It may be worth speaking to other parents first who would probably be glad of a universal time so that all the children are treated in a similar way.

You might consider setting some time aside each week for a family meeting to discuss how new rules are working out.

> *My five-year-old is going into hospital and is likely to be there for a few weeks. She's only just started school so this is likely to put her behind right from the start. She's also very nervous of the operation. What about her confidence?*

Preparing your child well for any new situation can help preserve confidence. She will feel less nervous if she knows exactly what to expect, so don't fall into the trap of glossing over the operation so as not to upset her. Get a book out of the library about going into hospital and look at it together, answering her questions honestly. Try to take a trip to the hospital and even visit the ward where she will be staying. If you are not intending to stay in hospital with her, explain that you will be visiting a lot and will have a treat lined up for her when she comes home. Play at hospitals with her teddies and dolls, perhaps giving a doll the operation your daughter is going to have. Find out as much as possible about it yourself so that you can explain it all to your child.

Talk to your child's teacher to reassure yourself that she will not get left behind. Perhaps there are some games to play or books to look at which will help. She may not feel well enough to do these at first, but perhaps while she is convalescing at home she could do some activities recommended by the teacher. Explain to the teacher how nervous your daughter is as she may be able to talk about the visit at school with the whole class. I am sure the teacher will encourage the other children to make cards or even visit your daughter so that she is happy to return to her school after the long break. You are bound to feel anxious yourself but try not to show it in front of your child. She will gain a lot from having confident adults around her.

> *I've tried praising my child but whenever I do she just contradicts me as if she thinks I'm making it up. She puts herself down at every opportunity.*

This is a sign of very poor self-esteem or self-image. Your child needs her confidence boosting so do keep the praise up even if you get a negative response. Whenever possible, turn her put-downs into positive remarks. For example, if she says 'I'm so useless, I just can't do it!' you might reply 'You're normally very good at that task – remember last time? Let's see if we can have a go together – two heads are better than one.' Whenever possible, praise your child for things which she cannot deny or reject. Set her easy tasks or give her more opportunities to use the talents she does have. It is also important to make sure that you are not the only one dishing up the praise. So enlist the help of the rest of the family, friends and even her school teacher.

> *My six-year-old still sucks her thumb. Is this a sign of poor confidence?*

Thumb sucking along with other childhood habits is just that – a habit. It almost certainly started as a comforter and may still operate like that, becoming more likely when your child is tired and in need of comfort. Stressful or difficult situations may also make thumb sucking more likely but avoiding them will not get rid of the thumb sucking. It has to be treated as a habit. Of course, if you wait long enough your child may stop of her own accord as she will not want to appear babyish in front of her friends. However, you can encourage her to give it up, if she wants to, with a star chart. Most children of this age do it only rarely during the day anyway so you must ask yourself how much of a problem it really is.

> *My teenager cannot make any decisions. He puts them off whenever possible and refuses to discuss the future. What is he worried about?*

Your child may well lack confidence, resulting in a fear of future events. Perhaps he has a fear of failure and prefers to avoid situations where failure is likely. Get your teenager to write down his thoughts about any major decision and then talk them through with you or another adult. It may be that he needs help with setting goals, but make sure he breaks these goals down into small achievable stages – having a major goal to achieve years ahead can be very daunting.

Always be positive about the future – your teenager is surrounded by negative images of unemployment and unhappiness. Make sure that you see his future in a very positive light without being too specific. Perhaps he feels a certain path is expected of him so ensure he knows that any decisions are his alone, although you are there to listen and help.

> *My twelve-year-old is very overweight and is getting teased at school. I don't know if it bothers her or not.*

Being different from other children can affect confidence and so can being bullied or teased. Your child is certainly at risk so keep an eye out for the signs. Is your child happy to go to school? Does she ever try to avoid certain activities such as swimming? Does she invite friends round and get invited back? Has her behaviour at home changed recently? Does she seem unusually moody? Does she still take care of her appearance? Does she spend more than her usual time alone in her room? Does she seem in any way depressed? Has she stopped going out to a regular club?

If your child seems to have none of the signs of poor self-esteem and appears outwardly confident, then you will not want to make a big thing of her weight. However, this is something which could affect her in the future so it still requires some thought. Firstly you need to consider why she is overweight. Does she eat impulsively, perhaps as a comfort? This in itself is a sign of low confidence. Or are you as a family overweight? Do you all take some form of exercise? You could help your child quite indirectly by ensuring that there are plenty of healthy foods such as fruit to pick at in times of hunger. At the same time you could cut down on the amount of sweet things you buy. Perhaps the whole family could take up a sport or form of exercise so that your child is not being singled out. You could put the emphasis on healthy eating and living rather than weight.

If your child does have a poor self-esteem and is being affected by the teasing, which is likely, then you may want to take a more direct line. However, you must praise your child for other things, including other aspects of her physical appearance, while tackling the weight problem. Help your child to set realistic goals with the help of your GP and, if appropriate, tackle your weight at the same time. However, the emphasis can still be put on healthy eating rather than diet.

‘ *What is school phobia? Is it just truancy?* ’

School phobia is literally a fear of going to school. This is not to be confused with anxiety about leaving you or straightforward truancy, although in some cases the underlying cause of school phobia and truancy may be the same. Firstly you would need to see if there is a reason for the phobia and the two most obvious reasons to consider are bullying or failure. Both of these can be tackled so that the phobia then goes. There may be a seemingly minor cause such as a fear of the dark cloakroom or an intense dislike of school dinners. So, if a cause can be found so much the better. In some cases there is no obvious cause and so it must be treated like any other phobia – your child must confront it in gradual stages. In some cases a child is fine when she gets there but it is the thought of school which panics her. Discuss it with the school so that the easiest drop-off is used – in some cases it may be helpful to take your child directly into the classroom; in other cases it may work to take your child in a few minutes late so that there is no anxious build up. Gradually work towards a more normal drop-off and praise your child for all her achievements.

> *My child has always been shy. The thought of moving up to secondary school seems to be making her even more withdrawn.*

Knowing what to expect should help your child's confidence so if her current school has not arranged a visit then you should. Try to introduce your child to some children who are already there so that she can find out even more about it. Talk to your child about the move as there may be something specific which is concerning her. Talk about secondary school in a very positive light – it is all too easy to focus on the exams and increased homework. Find out about the sporting facilities or anything else which may be of particular interest to your child. Help her to look on the move as something positive and get together with her friends who are moving too. She may not realise that she is not the only one who is apprehensive.

> *I was a latch-door kid – letting myself in after school and sometimes even getting myself up and ready for school in the morning. I want to make sure my children have a different start from me.*

It is natural for any parent to want the best for their children and in some cases to make sure they don't have to go through some of the traumas of their own childhood. However, it is important to keep this in perspective and not to over-compensate in any way. Of course you want to be there for your children but you must also allow them the independence they need. Confidence grows from gradually becoming more independent, and over-protection can stifle a child. Put your own childhood behind you and concentrate on the needs of your own children at each stage of their development.

> *I was smacked, made to respect my elders and betters and knew to be seen and not heard. It never did me any harm.*

Many adults come through difficult childhoods seemingly unscathed. Some even claim to have gained from it. Perhaps you had a very loving environment despite the smacking. Even so, do take a good hard look at yourself and ask the opinion of your partner too. Did it at any time affect your confidence, either as a child or a young adult? The chances are it did, if you are honest with yourself. You also have to remember that times have changed. Children now are given far more respect and this is in addition to discipline, not instead of it. Put your own childhood behind you and consider the needs of your children at each stage of their development, always looking for ways to boost confidence and self-esteem. No doubt you did gain from a secure discipline but you can give this to your own children without knocking their confidence or removing their self-respect.

> ‘*I am so glad my daughter has the confidence to do drama. I always wanted to be an actor and it looks like she's going that way too.*’

This is fine if it is what your daughter has chosen. Do, however, make sure that you are not living your ambitions through your child. Does she have the maturity and confidence to know her own mind or is she just trying to please you? Help your child come to decisions about her future without influencing her too much.

> ‘*My daughter and I do everything together – shopping, going to the cinema, choosing new clothes. She's my best friend.*’

Do make sure that your daughter has plenty of opportunity to socialise with friends of her own age and without feeling guilty that she is not spending the time with you. It may be that you are focusing all your life on her and this can act as pressure on her to succeed or act as you want her to. Being able to talk openly to you – which may be one aspect of your relationship – is very good for confidence. But being under pressure from you will have an adverse effect. Find yourself some interests away from your daughter and encourage her to do the same. Do enjoy your times together but make sure she is also able to act independently from you and can make some of her own decisions as she gets older without consulting you. Friendship is part of being a parent but you are a parent first and your daughter needs a different sort of relationship from that which she has with her peers. However, as she grows older, the parenting part diminishes and the friendship part can come to the fore.

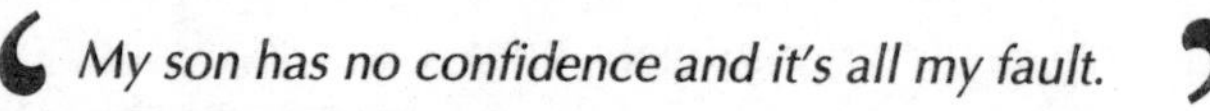

My son has no confidence and it's all my fault.

Although this book has put the emphasis on what you can do as a parent to help your child be confident, it does not follow that if he lacks confidence it is all your fault. Confidence comes from many factors including the personality your child was born with as well as past experiences and other relationships outside the home. Feeling guilty about your son's shyness or lack of confidence does not help. In fact, your child may even sense your guilt and get the message that you do not like him as he is. Of course you love him as he is and would not want to change him. So tell him, but at the same time feel positive and act. Boost his confidence now. It's never too late.

Useful addresses

UK

BRITISH ACTIVITY HOLIDAY ASSOCIATION, 22 Green Lane, Hersham, Walton on Thames, Surrey KT12 5HD. Tel: 01932 252994.

BRITISH ASSOCIATION OF ART THERAPISTS, 11A Richmond Road, Brighton, East Sussex BN2 3RL.

BRITISH ASSOCIATION FOR AUTOGENIC TRAINING AND THERAPY, 18 Holtsmere Road, Garston, Watford, Hertfordshire WD2 6NG.

BRITISH ASSOCIATION FOR DRAMA THERAPISTS, The Old Mill, Tolpuddle, Dorchester, Dorset DT2 7EX.

BRITISH REGISTER OF COMPLEMENTARY PRACTITIONERS, Institute for Complementary Medicine, PO Box 194, London SE16 1QZ. Tel: 0171 237 5165.

BRITISH STAMMERING ASSOCIATION, 15 Old Ford Road, London E2 6PJ. Tel: 0181 981 8818.

CRUSE (BEREAVEMENT CARE), Local group information from local citizen's advice bureau or telephone 0181 332 7227.

EATING DISORDERS ASSOCIATION, Sackville Place, 44–48 Magdalen Street, Norwich, Norfolk NR3 1JU. Tel: 01603 621414.

EXPLORING PARENTHOOD, 194 Freston Road, London W10 6TT. Tel: 0181 960 1678.

GINGERBREAD, 49 Wellington Street, London WC2E 7BN.

HOME START, 2 Falisbury Road, Leicester LE1 7QR. Tel: 01533 554988.

KIDSCAPE, 152 Buckingham Palace Road, London SW1 9TR. Tel: 0171 730 3300.

LABAN CENTRE FOR MOVEMENT AND DANCE, Laurie Grove, New Cross, London SE14 6NH. Tel: 0181 692 4070.

LET'S FACE IT, 10 Wood End, Crowthorne, Berks. Tel: 01344 774405.

NAEVUS SUPPORT GROUP, 58 Necton Road, Wheathampstead, St Albans, Hertfordshire AL4 8AU. Tel: 0158 283 2853.

NATIONAL ASSOCIATION FOR GIFTED CHILDREN, Park Campus, Boughton Green Road, Northampton NN2 7AL. Tel: 01604 792300.

NATIONAL STEPFAMILY ASSOCIATION, Chapel House, 18 Hatton Place, London EC1N 8RV.

PARENT NETWORK/PARENTLINK, 44–46 Caversham Road, London NW5 2DS. Tel: 0171 485 8535.

RELATE, Herbert Gray College, Little Church Street, Rugby CV21 3AP. Tel: 01788 573241.

RELAXATION FOR LIVING, 29 Burwood Park Road, Walton On Thames, Surrey KT12 5LH.

SELF-ESTEEM NETWORK, 32 Carisbrooke Road, London E17 7EF.

STEPFAMILY, 72 Willesden Lane, London NW6 7TA. Tel: 0171 372 0844.

Australia

AUSTRALIAN MARRIAGE COUNSELLING SERVICES, PO Box 55, 15 Hall Street, Lyneham, ACT 2602, Australia. Tel: 61–573273.

NATIONAL ASSOCIATION FOR GIFTED CHILDREN, University of New South Wales, PO Box 1, Kensington, New South Wales 2033, Australia.

SPEAKEASY ASSOCIATION, GPO Box 1173K, Melbourne, Victoria 3001, Australia.

Canada

FAMILY SERVICES, 55 Parkdale Avenue, Ottawa, K1Y 4G1, Canada.

SPEAKEASY INC., 95 Evergreen Avenue, St John, New Brunswick, E2N 1H4, Canada.

New Zealand

NEW ZEALAND SPEAKEASY ASSOCIATION, PO Box 18684, New Brighton, Christchurch 9, New Zealand.

RELATIONSHIP SERVICES, 6th Floor, Ansett House, 69–71 Bowlett Street, Wellington, New Zealand.

South Africa

SPEAKEASY STUTTERING ASSOCIATION, PO Box 55400, Northlands, Johannesburg, South Africa.

USA

NATIONAL ASSOCIATION FOR GIFTED CHILDREN, USA, Teachers College, Columbia University, New York, NY 10027, USA.

NATIONAL ASSOCIATION FOR RARE DISORDERS (including port-wine stains), 4610 Woodale Avenue, Edina, Minnesota 55424, USA. Tel: 2024796694.

NATIONAL STUTTERING PROJECT, 5100 East La Palma Avenue, Anahein, California 92807, USA.

Index

A

B

C

D

P

R

S

T

To order this series

All books in this series are available from your local bookshop or, in case of difficulty, can be ordered direct from the publisher. Just fill in the form below. Prices and availability subject to change without notice.

To: Hodder & Stoughton Ltd, Cash Sales Department, Bookpoint, 78 Milton Park, Abingdon. OXON, OX14 4TD, UK. If you have a credit card you may order by telephone – 01235 831700.

Please enclose a cheque or postal order made payable to Bookpoint Ltd to the value of the cover price and allow the following for postage and packing: UK & BFPO: £1.00 for the first book, 50p for the second book and 30p for each additional book ordered up to a maximum charge of £3.00. OVERSEAS & EIRE: £2.00 for the first book, £1.00 for the second book and 50p for each additional book.

Please send me

	copies of 0 340 60797 1	Prepare Your Child for School	£5.99	£
	copies of 0 340 60796 3	Help Your Child Through School	£6.99	£
	copies of 0 340 54750 2	Your Child From 5–11	£5.99	£
	copies of 0 340 57526 3	Talking and Your Child	£5.99	£
	copies of 0 340 60768 8	Help Your Child with Reading and Writing	£6.99	£
	copies of 0 340 60767 X	Help Your Child with Maths	£6.99	£
	copies of 0 340 60766 1	Help Your Child with a Foreign Language	£6.99	£
	copies of 0 340 64764 7	Your Child with Special Needs 2nd edition	£6.99	£
	copies of 0 340 62106 0	Teenagers in the Family	£5.99	£
	copies of 0 340 62105 2	Teenagers and Sexuality	£5.99	£
	copies of 0 340 65866 5	Help Your Child with Homework and Exams	£5.99	£
	copies of 0 340 66936 5	Help Your Child Through the National Curriculum	£6.99	£
			TOTAL	£

Name ....

Address ....

....

....Post Code ....

If you would prefer to pay by credit card, please complete:

Please debit my Visa/Access/Diner's Card/American Express (delete as appropriate) card no:

☐ ☐ ☐ ☐ ☐ ☐ ☐ ☐ ☐ ☐ ☐ ☐ ☐ ☐ ☐ ☐

Signature .... Expiry Date..

For sales in the following countries please contact:
UNITED STATES: Trafalgar Square (Vermont), Tel: 800 423 4525 (toll-free)
CANADA: General Publishing (Ontario), Tel: 445 3333
AUSTRALIA: Hodder & Stoughton (Sydney), Tel: 02 638 5299

Positive Parenting Reviews

'Written simply, in a straightforward style, with snippets of humour, this book is a must for any parent' on *Talking and Your Child* **Therapy Weekly**

'This new series can only help' on series **The Northern Echo**

'Offers practical advice and information and covers all areas that concern parents' on *Prepare Your Child for School* **Parents Magazine**

'Once you've bought the latest two books in the series, there really will be no excuse not to be prepared for anything!' on *Prepare Your Child for School* and *Help Your Child Through School* **Nursery World**

'This will be very popular. It deals with parents' major worries in a firm, but calm reassuring tone, contains some useful advice and addresses and there are some excellent ideas for activities and games to encourage various areas of development' on *Prepare Your Child for School* **Education Review**

'The advice is down-to-earth, the practical activities are well-balanced and there is a useful section on books: an excellent insight into what should be done and why' on *Help Your Child with Reading and Writing* **Nursery World**

'This series looks like it's set to fill the gap in the mass of babycare books available' on series **Parents Magazine**

'Susan Kerr's thoughtful, sympathetic, yet never sentimental handbook is a treasure for all parents. It contains clear, practical, level-headed advice on how to cope; it is well written, well-researched, often amusing, and of enormous help to any parents, as well as to parents of special needs children' on *Your Child With Special Needs* **Women Writers' Network**

'Clearly structured with many good ideas, the instructions for games are carefully and concisely written' on *Help Your Child with Maths* **The British Journal of Educational Psychology**

'Teacher trainees find this book very helpful and often say they will use the ideas in it to improve their own public relations and information to parents. I recommend this book as a working tool' on *Teach Your Child a Foreign Language* **Authentically English**